In the Mind's Eye

Lucy Grealy is a poet who was born in Dublin in 1963. She moved with her family to America in 1967. Her poems have appeared, among other places, in *The Paris Review* and the *TLS*. She has been awarded a number of prizes and honours including the *Times Literary Supplement* Poetry prize.

In the Mind's Eye

Lucy Grealy

ARROW

First published in Arrow in 1995

1 3 5 7 9 10 8 6 4 2

© Lucy Grealy 1994

First published in the United Kingdom in 1994 by
Century, 20 Vauxhall Bridge Road, London SW1V 2SA

Arrow Books Limited
Random House, 20 Vauxhall Bridge Road, London SW1V 2SA

Random House Australia (Pty) Limited
20 Alfred Street, Milsons Point, Sydney,
New South Wales 2061, Australia

Random House New Zealand Limited
18 Poland Road, Glenfield
Auckland 10, New Zealand

Random House South Africa (Pty) Limited
PO Box 337, Bergvlei, South Africa

Random House UK Limited Reg. No. 954009

A CIP catalogue record for this book
is available from the British Library

ISBN 0 09 932701 5

Printed and bound in Great Britain by
Cox & Wyman Ltd, Reading, Berkshire

In memory of my father

Desmond Delargy Grealy
(1921–1979)

Contents

Prologue
Pony Party

MY FRIEND STEPHEN and I used to do pony parties together. The festivities took place on the well-tended lawns of the vast suburban communities which had sprung up around the rural acres of Diamond E stables. Mrs Evans, the owner of Diamond E, took advantage of these opportunities and readily dispatched a couple of ponies for birthday parties. In the early years, Mrs Evans used to attend the parties with us, something Stephen and I dreaded. She fancied herself a sort of Mrs Roy Rogers and dressed in embarrassing accordance: fringe shirts, oversized belt buckles, ramshackle hats. I'd stand there holding a pony, cringing inwardly with mortification as if she were my own mother. But as we got older and Stephen got his driver's licence, and as Diamond E itself slowly sank into a somewhat surreal, muddy and orphaned state of anarchy, we worked the parties by ourselves, something I relished.

We were invariably late for the birthday parties, a result of loading the ponies at the last minute, combined with our truly remarkable propensity for getting lost. I never really minded, though, enjoying the drive through those precisely planned streets as the summer air swirled through the pick-up's cab, rustling the crepe-paper ribbons temporarily draped over the rear-view mirror. When we'd finally found our destination, we'd clip the ribbons into the ponies' manes and tails in a rather sad attempt to imbue a festive air. The neighbourhoods themselves were varied with everything from close, tree-laden streets crammed in with ranch-style houses to more spacious boulevards dotted with outsized Tudors. Still, all the neighbourhoods in Rockland County seemed to share a certain carbon-copy quality: house after house looked exactly like the one before it save for the occasional cement deer or sculpted shrub. Invariably, a dog would always appear, chasing the trailer for what seemed like a set number of lawns, some mysterious canine demarcation of territory, before suddenly dropping away, only to be replaced by another one running and barking behind us a few lawns later.

I liked those dogs, their sense of purpose and enjoyment and responsibility. I especially liked being lost, tooling through strange neighbourhoods with Stephen. As we drove by the houses, I gazed into the windows imagining what the families inside were like. My ideas were loosely based on what I had learned from TV and films: I pictured a father in a reclining chair next to a lamp, its shade trimmed with a row of small white tassels. Somewhere, nearby, a wife in a matched outfit chatted on the phone with friends as their children set the dinner table. As they passed the home-cooked meal around in assorted white serving dishes, they'd casually ask each other about their day. Perhaps someone might even mention the unusual sight of a horse trailer going past the house that day. Certain these families were nothing like my own, this certainty wrought with a sense of vague superiority and even vaguer longing, I prided myself with the pleasure of knowing that I was the person in that strangely surreal trailer with the kicking ponies and angry muffler, that I had driven by their house that day, that I had brushed against their lives, and past them, like that.

Once we reached our destination, there was a great rush of excitement. The children, realizing that the ponies had arrived, would come running from the back yard in their silly hats, as their now forgotten balloons, bobbing colourfully behind them, would fly off in search of some tree or telephone wire. The ponies, reacting to the excitement of the new sounds and smells, would promptly take a crap right there in the driveway, which in turn was greeted by a chorus of disgusted groans.

My pleasure at the sight of the children didn't last for very long, however. I knew what was coming. As soon as they got over the thrill of being near the ponies, they'd notice me. Half my jaw was missing and it gave my face a strange, triangular shape accentuated by the fact I was unable to keep my mouth properly closed. When I first started doing pony parties my hair was still short and wispy, still growing out from the chemo. But as it grew I made things worse by continuously bowing my head and hiding behind the curtain of hair, furtively peering out at the world like some nervous actor. Unlike the actor, though, I didn't secretly relish my audience, and if it were possible I'd have stood behind that curtain forever, my head bent in an eternal act of deference. I was, however, dependent upon my audience. It was their approval or disapproval which defined everything, and, unfortunately, I believed with every cell in my body that approval wasn't written into my particular script. I was fourteen years old.

'I *hate* this, why am I doing this?' I'd ask myself each and every outing, but I had no choice if I was going to keep my job at the stable. Everyone had to do pony parties; no exceptions. Years later a friend remarked how odd it was that an adult would even think to send a disfigured child to work at a kid's party, but at the time it was never an issue. If my very presence in these back yards was something of an anomaly it wasn't just because of my face. In fact, my physical oddness seemed somehow to fit in with the general oddness and failings of Diamond E.

It was a small place, near the bottom of a gently sloping hill. Each spring when the snow melted, it left an ankle-deep mud behind that wouldn't completely dry up until mid-summer. Mrs Evans possessed a number of peculiar traits which made life at Diamond E unpredictable. When she wasn't trying to save our souls, or treating Stephen's rumoured homosexuality by unexpectedly exposing her breasts to him, she was taking us on shoplifting sprees, dropping her criminal hints like some Artful Dodger.

No one at Diamond E had any real idea of how to care for horses properly. Most of the animals were kept outside in three small, grassless corrals. The barn was on the verge of collapse; every entrance into it was accompanied by the fluttering sound of startled rats. The 'staff' consisted of a bunch of junior and high school kids willing to work in exchange for riding privileges. And the main source of income, apart from pony parties, was hacking; renting out the horses for ten dollars an hour to anyone willing to pay. The horses themselves were bought at an auction whose main customer was the meat dealer for a dog-food company: Diamond E, more often than not, was merely a way station. The general air of neglect surrounding the stable was more a result of ignorance than apathy. It's not as if we didn't care, we simply didn't know any better. And, for most of us, especially me, Diamond E was a haven. Though I had to suffer the pony parties, it was a price I was more than willing to pay just to spend time alone with the horses. I considered animals bearers of higher truth, and I wanted to align myself with their knowledge. I thought animals were the only beings capable of understanding me.

The chemotherapy had ended only months before I started looking for stables where I might work. Just fourteen and still unaware of the exact details of my surgery, I made my way down the yellow pages. It was the July Fourth weekend and Mrs Evans, typically overbooked, said I had called at exactly the right moment. Overjoyed, I went into the kitchen to tell my mother I had a job at a stable. She looked at me dubiously.

'Did you tell them about yourself?'

I hesitated, and lied. 'Yes, of course I did.'

'Are you sure they know you were sick? Will you be up for this?'

'Of *course* I am,' I replied in my most petulant, adolescent tone of voice.

In actuality, it had never even occurred to me to mention cancer, or my face, to Mrs Evans. I was still blissfully unaware, somehow believing that the only reason people stared at me was because my hair was still growing out. And so, my mother, unwitting of the world I was about to enter, obligingly drove all sixty-odd pounds of me down to Diamond E, where my pale and misshapen face seemed to surprise all of us. They let me water a few horses, imagining I wouldn't last more than a day. I stayed for four years.

The first day I walked a small piebald in circle after circle, practically drunk with the aroma of the horses. But with each circle, each new child lifted into the tiny saddle, I became more and more uncomfortable with myself, and with each circuit my head dropped just a little bit further in shame. With time I became adept at handling the horses, and even more so at avoiding the direct stares of the children.

As our trailer pulled into each driveway I would briefly remember my own excitement of being around ponies for the first time. But I also knew that these children lived apart from me. Through them I learned the language of paranoia: every whisper I heard was a whisper about the way I looked; every laugh, a joke at my expense.

Partly, I was honing my self-consciousness into a torture device, sharp and efficient enough to last me the rest of my life. Partly, I was right: they *were* staring at me, laughing at me. The cruelty of children is immense, almost startling in its precision. The kids at the parties were fairly young and, as they were surrounded by adults, rarely made cruel remarks outright. But to me, their open, uncensored stares were more painful than the deliberate comments from peers at school, where insecurities drove everything and everyone like some looming, evil presence in a haunted machine. But in those back yards, where the grass was mown so short and sharp it would have hurt to walk upon it, there was only the fact of me, my face, my ugliness.

This singularity of meaning – I *was* my face, I *was* ugliness – though sometimes unbearable, also offered a possible point of escape. It became the launching pad from which to lift off, the one immediately recognizable place to point to when asked what was wrong with my life. Everything led to it, everything receded from it – my own face as personal vanishing point. The pain these children brought with their stares engulfed every other pain in my life. Yet, occasionally, just as that vast ocean threatened to swallow me whole, it was as if some greater force lifted me out and enabled me to walk amongst them as easily, as carelessly, and as alien as the pony which trotted beside me, his tail held high in excitement, his nostrils wide with anticipation of a brief encounter with a world beyond his comprehension.

The parents were a different story. When we arrived they'd trail behind the kids, iced drinks clinking, making their own, more practical comments about the fresh horse manure on their driveway. If Stephen and I liked the look of them (for all our judgements were instantaneous), we'd shovel it up; if not, we'd tell them clean-up wasn't part of the fee. Stephen came from a large, all-American family, but for me these grown-ups provided secret fascination. The women wore frosted lipstick and long bright fingernails; the fathers sported gold watches and smelled of too much aftershave.

This was the late seventies and a number of corporate head-quarters had sprung up over the New Jersey border. Complete with duck ponds and fountains, these 'industrial parks' looked more like fancy hotels than office buildings, and the newly planted suburban lawns I found myself parading ponies on were a direct result of their proliferation. They also managed to reinforce my feelings of being an outsider by reminding me of what my own family didn't have: money.

My family *should* have had money: this was true in practical terms (my father was a successful journalist), and also true within our family mythology which summoned up images of Fallen Aristocracy. We were displaced foreigners, Europeans newly arrived in an alien landscape. If we actually had the money we felt entitled to, we would never have spent it on anything as mundane as a house in Spring Valley, or on anything as silly and trivial as a pony party.

Unfortunately, all of the mythologically endowed money didn't materialize. Despite my father's good job with a major television network, we were barraged by collection agencies while our house was literally falling apart around us. Either unwilling or unable, I'm not sure which, to spend money on proper plumbers and electricians and general handymen, my father turned handyman himself. Our house was barely held together by a complex system of odd bits of wire, duct tape and putty, all applied rather haphazardly and good-naturedly by him on weekend afternoons. He sang when he worked. Bits of opera slapped jauntily together with the current top forty and ancient ditties from his childhood, all of which were periodically interrupted so that he might patiently explain his work to the dog, who always listened attentively.

Anything my father fixed generally did not stay fixed for more than a few months. Our toilets, when it rained, needed to be coaxed with a zen-like ritual of jiggles in order to flush without spilling the entire contents of the septic tank onto the basement floor. One walked by the oven door with a sense of near reverence, lest it would fall open with an operatic crash. Pantheism ruled.

Similarly, when dealing with my mother, one always had to act in a delicate and prescribed way, though the exact rules of protocol seemed to shift frequently and without advance notice. One day, running out of milk was easily dealt with, while on the next it was a symbol of her children's selfishness, our father's failure, and her tragic, wasted life. Money, or so it was driven into us, was the root of all our unhappiness. So as Stephen and I drove through those 'bourgeois' suburbs (my radical older brothers had taught me to identify them as such), I genuinely believed that if our family were as well off as these families, the extra carton of milk would not have been an issue, and my mother would have been more than delighted to buy gallon after gallon until the house fairly spilled over with fresh milk.

Though our whole family shared the burden of my mother's anger, in my heart I suspected that part of it was my fault and my fault alone. Cancer is an obscenely expensive illness; I saw the bills, I heard their fights. There was no doubt that I was personally responsible for a great deal of my family's money problems; ergo, I was responsible for my mother's unhappy life. During the many fights my parents had over money I would sit in the kitchen in silence, unable to move even after my brothers and sisters had fled to their bedrooms. I sat there listening as some kind of penance.

The parents who presided over the pony parties never fought, or at least not about anything significant, of this I felt sure. Resentment made me scorn them, their gauche houses and spoiled children. These feelings might have been purely political like those of my left-wing brothers, whose actual philosophies I understood very little of, if it weren't for the painfully personal detail of my face.

'What's wrong with her face?'

The mothers bent down to hear this question and, still bent over, they'd look over at me, their glances refracting away as quickly and predictably as light through a prism. I couldn't always hear their response, but knew from experience vague pleas for politeness would hardly satisfy a child's curiosity.

While the eyes of their children bored swiftly and deftly into the deepest part of me, the glances from the parents provided me with an exotic sense of power as I watched them inexpertly pretend not to notice me. I led their perfectly formed children around on the backs of ponies, children only a couple of years younger than I was when I got cancer at the age of nine.

As I passed the swing sets once more, looped around to pick up the next child waiting near the picnic table littered with cake plates, juice bottles and party favours, I'd pause there, confrontational like some Dickensian ghost, imagining that my very presence served as an uneasy reminder of what might be. What had happened to me was any parent's nightmare, and I allowed myself to believe that my very presence was dangerous to them. The parents obliged me in this: they brushed past me, around me, sometimes even smiled at me. But not once in the three or so years that I worked pony parties, ever asked me directly what had happened.

They were uncomfortable because of my face. I ignored the deep hurt by allowing the side of me which was desperate for any kind of definition, to staunchly act out, if not exactly relish, this macabre status.

Zoom lenses, fancy flash systems, perfect focus – it didn't escape my notice that these cameras were probably worth more than the very ponies instigating the pictures. A physical sense of dread took over as soon as I spotted the thickly padded case, heard the sound of the zipper, noted the ridiculous, almost surgical protectiveness with which the instrument was taken out of its fitted foam compartment. I'd automatically hold onto the pony's halter, careful to keep his head tight and high in case he should suddenly pull down for a bite of lawn. Or else I'd expertly turn my own head away, pretending I was only just then aware of something more important off to the side, causing me to tilt away at exactly the same angle each time, my hair falling in a perfect sheet of camouflage between me and the camera. I stood there, perfectly still, just as I had sat for the countless medical photographs: full face, turn to the left, the right, now a three-quarter shot to the left. I took a certain pride in knowing the routine so well. I've even seen some of these medical photographs in publications. Curiously, those sterile, bright photos are easy for me to look at. For one thing, I know that only doctors look at them, perhaps I'm even slightly proud that I'm such an interesting case, worthy of documentation. Or maybe I do not really think it is me, sitting there, *Case 3, figure number 6-A*.

Once, when my doctor left me waiting too long in his examining room, I leafed through my file, which I knew was strictly off-limits. I was thrilled to find a whole section of slides housed in their own clear plastic folder. Removing one, I lifted it up to the fluorescent light, stared for a moment, then carefully, calmly replaced it. It had been a photograph taken of me on the operating table. Most of the skin of the right side of my face had been pulled over and back, exposing something with the vague shape of a face and neck but with the colour and consistency of raw steak. A clamp gleamed off to the side, holding something unidentifiable in place. I wasn't particularly bothered; I've always had a fascination with gore and had it been someone else I'd have stared endlessly, but in this case I simply put it back in its appropriate slot and made a mental note not to look at slides from my file again, ever.

With the same numbed yet cavalier stance, I would wait for a father to click the shutter. At least these were photographs I'd never have to see, though to this day I fantasize about meeting someone who eventually shows me their photo album and there, in the middle of a page, is me, inexplicably holding a pony. There is only one pony party photo of me I've actually seen. In it, I'm holding onto a small dark bay pony whose name I don't remember. I look frail and thin and certainly peculiar, but I don't look anywhere near as repulsive as I remember believing I did. There's a gaggle of children around me, waiting for their turn on the pony. My stomach was always in knots then, surrounded by so many children, but I can tell by my expression that I'm convincing myself I don't care as I point to the back of the line. The children look older than most of the kids from the back-yard parties: some of them are even older than nine, the age I was when I got sick. I'm probably thinking about this, too, as I order them into line.

I can still hear the rubbery, metallic thud of hooves on the trailer's ramp, the sound which always heralded the final act as we loaded the ponies back into the hot and smelly box for the ride back to Diamond E. Fifteen years later, when I see that photo of me, I am filled with questions I rarely allow myself, such as how we go about turning into the people we were meant to be. What relation do the human beings in that picture have now to the ones they were then? How is it that all of us were caught together in that brief moment of time, me standing there pretending I wasn't hurt by a single thing in this world while they lined up for their turn on the pony, some of them excited and some of them scared, but all of them neatly, at my insistence, one in front of the other, like all the days ahead?

I

Luck

=====

KER-POW! I was literally knocked into the present, the unmistakable *now*, by Joni Friedman's head as it collided with the right side of my jaw. Up until that moment in time my body had been existing in the same space, running around within the confines of a circle of fourth grade children gathered for a game of dodge-ball, but my mind had been elsewhere. For the most part, I was an abysmal athlete and was deeply embarrassed whenever I failed to jump bravely and deftly into a whirring jumprope, ever threatening to sting for mis-crossing its invisible boundaries like some science-fiction forcefield, or worse when I was the weak link yet again in the school relay race. How could one doubt that the order in which one was picked for the softball team was anything but concurrent with the order in which Life would be handing out favours?

Not that I considered myself a weak or easily frightened person; in more casual games I excelled, especially at wrestling (I could beat every boy but one on my street), playing war (I was always called upon to be the scout because I was a known sneak), and in taking dares (I would do just about anything, no matter how ludicrous or dangerous, except for eating non-vertebrates and amphibians, which was where I drew the line). There was a certain amount of respect accorded me in my neighbourhood, not only because I once jumped out of a second-storey window, but because I also would kiss an old and particularly smelly neighbourhood dog on the lips whenever asked. I was a tomboy par excellence.

But when games turned official under the auspices of the Fleetwood Elementary Phys-Ed department, everything changed.

The minute a whistle appeared on the scene and boundaries were called I transformed into a *spaz*. It all seemed so unfair: I *knew* in my heart I had great potential, star potential even, but none of this actually translated into hitting whatever ball was coming my way. I resigned myself early on, even though I knew I could out-read, out-spell and out-test the strongest kid in the classroom. And when I was picked practically last for crazy-kickball or crab relays, I would defeatedly assume a certain lackadaisical attitude which partially accounts for my negligence on the day my jaw collided with Joni Friedman's head.

Even if I was more involved in wondering whether Colleen's superiority at dodge-ball was compromised by her all-consuming crush on David Cassidy, or if other social dilemmas of pre-pubescence ruled that day's game of dodge-ball, I do know that the ball I was going for was *mine*. I hadn't even bothered to call it, it was so obvious, and though it was also obvious Joni was going to try and steal it away from me, I stood my ground. The whistle to stop playing began to blow just as the ball came towards us, towards me. I leaned forward and Joni lunged sideways and suddenly any and all thoughts about Colleen's social status or Joni's ethics were suddenly and sharply knocked out of me.

I felt the force of our collision in every one of my atoms, though calmly and lucidly as I sat there slightly dazed on the asphalt. Everyone was running to get on line and though I assume Joni asked me how I was, I only remember sitting there amongst the blurred and running legs, rubbing the right side of my jaw, utterly fascinated both by how much pain I was in and by how strangely peaceful I felt. It wasn't that things were happening in slow motion, a sensation I had experienced during other minor accidents; it was as if time had mysteriously though logically shifted onto another plane. It felt as if I could speculate and theorize about a thousand different beautiful truths all in the same amount of time it would take my lips to form a single word. In retrospect, it's possible I had a concussion.

My jaw throbbed. Rubbing it with my hand seemed to have no effect either way: the pain was deep and untouchable. Because the pain was genuinely unanticipated there was no residue of anxiety to alter my experience of it. Anxiety and anticipation, I soon learned, were the most essential ingredients in *suffering* from pain, as opposed to feeling pain, pure and simple. This alien ache was, probably, the first and last time I was to experience such unadulterated pain, which perplexed me more than actually hurt me.

'Are you alright, dear?'

Interrupted in my twilight, I looked up to see Mrs Minkin, who was on playground duty that afternoon. She fell into the category of 'scary' adults, and from there into the sub-category of adults 'with cooties'. Mrs Minkin, a woman luridly ugly to school-children's eyes in her plaid wool skirts and thick make-up, was not someone to whom I was willing to admit distress.

'I'm fine, thank you.'

And I was fine: as quickly as it had happened, the sharp ache in my jaw receded and my sense of self transported itself back to the playground where I quickly stood up and brushed myself off. The looming issue now was merely how far back in line I would have to stand because of this bothersome delay. By the time I was back in the classroom I had forgotten the incident entirely.

I was reminded of it again that evening as I sat on the living-room rug earnestly trying to whip up a book report I had been putting off for two weeks, which now, to my grave dismay, was due the very next day. Gradually, I became aware of possible salvation: I had a toothache. This wasn't as welcome a reason for staying home from school as a cold or other related illness was because it would entail a visit to the dentist. Had it been only a minor toothache I'd probably have preferred to suffer the wrath of my teacher over my mother's inevitable agitation, but now that I had noticed the ache it seemed to be progressing at a steady rate.

The dentist and I were already well acquainted. I was cursed with terrible teeth. We were told it is a common trait among people of Anglo-Irish descent, but my mother felt personally affronted by this bit of information and, as if by osmosis, I too felt a sense of shame about the state of my teeth. Dr Singer convinced my parents that if there was to be any chance at all of normal adult teeth growing in, he should be allowed, post-haste, to do everything imaginable to my baby teeth. I can't even remember the work he did, but it seemed as if I was going to the dentist every week to have some mysterious procedure applied to my mouth.

No one likes the dentist, yet what I resented most about Dr Singer was that he made a practice of lying to me.

'Hold out your thumb and I'll show you how I'll make your tooth go to sleep so that nothing will hurt it.'

I'd hold it out.

'You see, I'll put this medicine on your tooth just like I'm putting it on your thumb,' he'd say as he pushed a syringe lightly into my finger, releasing a jet of clear fluid.

'It won't hurt any more than that.'

Then he'd turn to his instrument tray, his back blocking my view, and switch syringes. Before I could see what flashed before me, he'd stick the needle deftly into my waiting gums. I was always so surprised that a simple stream of fluid could hurt that much. Even when he performed this dirty trick on me again and again, I concluded that there must be something extraordinarily wrong with my gums. I suspected some terrible problem in my mouth and, afraid complaining would only cause some new unknown and certainly painful treatment, I kept my doubts to myself.

As the evening wore on pretending the toothache wasn't there became less and less of an option. Finally I went to my mother and confessed my pain to her in the same guarded tone I might use to admit the loss or destruction of something valuable. As I expected, she was angry. Of course, she was angry at the situation, at the bother, at the possible cost, but I had no recourse at that age to the ability to distinguish such subtle gradations and painfully presumed her anger was directed at me and me alone.

My father walked into the room and asked what was going on. It was only then that I remembered my collision earlier in the day. This new information seemed to irritate my mother even more, especially when my father, characteristically trying to dissolve the tension of the situation, ventured the prognosis 'She's just got a cold in her tooth, that's all, she'll be fine in the morning.'

The intent was admirable enough, but his dismissing the problem only made the situation worse, confirming my mother's belief that she was the only one in the family who faced facts. This was actually true in a sense, but she never recognized that her anger scared all of us into retreat. By churning problems through her own personal mill, she kept us from ever discussing a problem outright, which, in turn, exacerbated the problem. My mother was always particularly annoyed when my father put on his good-fellow-Irishman act and dispensed comforting misinformation about the world, such as this backward notion that a tooth could have a cold in it. I was sent off to bed with two aspirin and a promise of reappraisal.

'You've got lock-jaw.'

My brothers pronounced this happily the next morning, obviously excited by the idea.

I mumbled back to them as best I could.

They were only too pleased to describe in detail how I could never open my mouth again, that everything I ever ate from now on could come to me only through a straw. Though it was true I had woken up with my jaw swollen and seemingly locked – it didn't hurt when I tried to open it as much as it appeared simply to be stuck – a diet of milkshakes didn't really seem like such an awful fate to me. Primarily, however, I was excited by the idea that something really *was* wrong with me, that I hadn't simply been overreacting the previous night as I had allowed myself to believe; I was bona fide sick; no school *definitely*. I was decidedly cheerful. My mother made an appointment for me to see the family doctor later that morning.

'Well, considering the swelling and this immobility, and that she had a hard knock, I'd say it's probably fractured.'

A broken jaw. This would be the first of many diagnoses and surely the one most utterly off course. Dr Cantor explained plainly to me that if it was broken I'd have to have it wired shut so it could heal, but first I had to go over to the hospital to have it x-rayed. I wasn't particularly thrilled with the wired-shut part, but I was too involved with the idea of venturing off to a hospital emergency room to give much thought to the latter step. I might have been frightened at the prospect if it weren't for the fact that my two absolute hands-down favourite television programmes were 'Emergency!' and 'Medical Center'. The possibility of personally getting to live out one of these thirty-minute dramas elated me. My mother kindly indulged me as I sat on a trolley in one of the curtained cubicles, humouring me about what an adventure it all was, how jealous my brothers would be that I was the principle player in such a drama. She told me how brave I was and how lucky we all were that this had happened to me and not Sarah, my twin sister and avowed scaredy-cat. Sarah would have cried horrendously had it been her sitting there, but not me, I was courageous and didn't cry and, thus, was good. It seemed a natural enough equation at the time.

The x-rays came back: it wasn't a broken jaw, but something called a dental cyst, probably caused when the force of the blow forced one of my back molars down into the gum, nicking the mandible. It was nothing serious, but they would have to operate to remove it right away to avoid an infection. I went back home with my mother to collect my pyjamas and off we went to Pascack Valley Hospital, a small community hospital in the next town over. Surgery was scheduled for the very next day.

What I remember most from that first night is that I didn't sleep very much, having devoted most of the time to a silly conversation with the girl in the bed across from me involving, of all things, David Cassidy. She was also particularly fascinated with how my temperature was taken throughout the night to monitor possible infection, a harmless enough procedure except for the fact that my nurse insisted on taking it rectally and on not bothering to draw the curtain, much to the viewing delight of my neighbour who stood up in her bed to watch. She giggled and I thought her a fool, but I didn't yet have enough recourse to dignity to do anything other than giggle at my absurd situation along with her. At midnight a nurse came along and taped an NPO sign to my bed: Nil Per Oral, nothing by mouth. I felt special, singled out, and allowed a condescending tone into my speech as I explained to my neighbour what it meant, having just had the nurse explain it to me thirty seconds before.

Each and every hospital has its own particular and quirky protocol. Some hospitals make you put on a surgical gown in your own room, some make you wait until you reach the operating room. Some anaesthetic departments have specific rooms in which you are put to sleep, others take you right on into the operating room itself. Pascack Valley Hospital subscribed to the latter and also, bless their hearts, to the theory that it's best to knock one's patient out as quickly as possible and *then* assign the various IVs and other assorted needles and tubes to their final bodily destinations. In medical terms this isn't the most desirable method, as ideally one should have instant access to the blood and airway systems should anything go suddenly awry during the initial stages of gas application, but presumably in this small paediatrics department they figured it wasn't worth all the tears, screams and struggling: get the conscious entity out of the way as quickly as possible, then insert instruments to your heart's content.

Still living within the fantasy of a television show and also slightly dopey both from the pre-med and from my sleepless night, I was duly impressed with the sight of a real live operating-room, just as I had been pleased by the eye-witness view of the corridor's ceiling during the trolley ride down there. I was somewhat disappointed when I failed to detect a glass domed amphitheatre through which row after row of doctors would peer down, intrigued by my fascinating case, but the gleaming metal and impressive lights, exactly as I'd anticipated, placated me. My first authentic surgically masked face peered down at me, blocking the bright light from the overhead lamp.

'I'm going to put this mask over your face and give you some air to make you sleepy, it might smell a little funny.'

Funny was an understatement: it was disgusting. Through the black rubber mask came the most alien, chemical fumes, so other to me that I could never have even presumed such a smell even existed. I thought I would suffocate. I struggled slightly, trying to turn my head away and reach for the mask with my hands. Someone I couldn't see reached out and grasped my hands, squeezing them too tightly while someone else put their hands on my forehead. This last gesture calmed me instantly.

'Now I want you to close your eyes and breathe and relax and think about some nice things. Do you have any pets?'

I began to list the names of the menagerie back home, aware that a faint buzzing was growing louder and louder. The things around me began to lose their borders. The doctor's face and the bodies of people hovering nearby no longer appeared in terms of what they were, but in terms of what they were not. It became increasingly difficult to speak. After listing only the names of two cats, I was reduced to producing only a syllable at a time with each breath, and even that seemed like a great deal of effort.

'Close your eyes.'

This was unthinkable. First, I didn't want to miss a thing, and second, what if they thought I was asleep and began cutting me open and I was merely resting my eyes? This last fear was to haunt me through subsequent operations. Even after I admitted my fear a couple of years later and had the whole process patiently explained, I still remained wary.

I felt nauseous. The gas was overpowering, although the mask seemed to have been removed from my face, the buzz now drowning everything else out and finally I couldn't take it any longer and rolled over to vomit. A magenta, viscous liquid with swirls of green poured out and created an interesting stain on the white sheet. I must have groaned because someone put a metal basin near me into which I vainly tried to deposit more of the smelly but curiously sweet concoction. I still felt nauseous but could bring nothing else up and lay back and closed my eyes, exhausted from the effort. A strange nurse was standing beside my bed insisting I acknowledge her first visually and then, to my great annoyance, verbally. The very last thing I wanted to do just then was to open my eyes, let alone speak to this woman, who, on top of everything else, was now asking the most ludicrous question I'd ever heard: Lucinda, what time is it? I wasn't used to people calling me by my full, given name. With an outstretched arm she directed my gaze over to a clock on the wall. This is ridiculous, I thought. Couldn't she understand that sleeping is the singly most desirable act in the world, the one and only thing I could ever want to do with the rest of my life? She asked me a third time and only to rid myself of her I gathered my wits and focusing powers and told her. It was eleven ten. My first operation was over.

Six months later, sometime near Easter, I came home from school with the right side of my face swollen and hot. I'd been going in to hospital sporadically to have x-rays of my jaw taken ever since the first surgery. A bony knob had appeared on the very tip of my jaw under my ear shortly after the initial surgery and my mother asked about it repeatedly.

'It's just a bony growth, it's nothing to worry about, Mrs Grealy.'

'But surely it's not normal for a young girl to have a lump like that on her face?'

'It's just a bony growth, Mrs Grealy, nothing unusual after such surgery.'

The doctor, who wasn't even a doctor but only a specialized dentist, smiled condescendingly after each inquiry. Nothing infuriated my mother more than this condescension, which even I recognized as endemic amongst the medical population. Unfortunately for my mother, I was still a typical nine-year-old and seized upon every possibility I could to be embarrassed by her. Why did she have to make such a fuss? Couldn't she just accept what they said? Not brave enough actually to speak up, I mentally rolled my eyes with each encounter between my mother and the doctor; if I'd ever suspected how classical and common my tendency was towards filial shame I'd have surely abandoned it and sided with my mother. I was vain and proud when it came to wanting to be different from everyone else. I wanted nothing more than to be special, and so far the role of patient had delivered. A noticeable amount of special treatment had been thrown my way by my teachers and I'd gained a new level of respect from my friends since having gone under the knife.

When my mother marched me back to Dr Cantor's office, it was almost with a sense of righteousness. It was obvious I had a bad infection which they could no longer ignore, and my heart thrilled when I heard the words emergency surgery used in conjunction with my name. They had to drain and clean out the almost visibly growing and angrier-by-the-minute looking lump on my face. I asked if I'd get to go to the hospital in an ambulance and was abjectly disappointed when told no.

As far as I was concerned I was still on a great adventure, the star of my own television special. Up until that point my greatest trial in life had been the emotional upheaval hovering over our painful family situation. This physical drama seemed a bit of light relief to me. Besides that, there was yet another unfinished book report looming. Just when I thought it was hopeless, I'd been handed yet again this brilliant stroke of luck. Something as impressive sounding as Emergency Surgery had to be worth as long an extension as I could ask for, as well as another round of presents in the offing. It seems odd to me now that a deed as relatively easy as not crying over a needle was rewarded so lavishly while my Herculean efforts simply not to fall apart during one of the many family crises went by completely unnoticed. The way I saw it, I was onto something good.

After the surgery my parents were instructed to take me to the Strang Clinic, which was translated down to me as a trip to the City. I was thrilled: I loved any chance at all to drive through those filthy, bewildering streets, see so many different types of people, marvel that so much noise could exist all at once, horns, sirens, human yells. It was there that we met the eccentric Dr John Conley, a leader in the field of head and neck surgery. After a thorough examination, arrangements were made to have me admitted to the children's wing within Columbia Presbyterian Hospital, known as Babies' Hospital.

When a film's heroine innocently coughs, you know that two scenes later, max, she'll be in an oxygen tent, or when a man bumps into a woman at the train station, you know that man will become the woman's lover and/or murderer. In everyday life, where we cough often and are always bumping into people, our daily actions rarely reverberate so lucidly. Though we probably thought little of it at the time, once we love or hate someone we can think back and remember the first casual time we saw them. But what are we to make of all the chance meetings that nothing ever comes of? While our bodies exist and move ever forward on the time line, our minds continuously traject backward, seeking shape and meaning as deftly as any arrow seeking its mark.

As I sat there on the playground's sticky asphalt I experienced time in a new way, but perhaps the significance of that memory depends on the way my life has unfolded. It seems so odd and almost uncanny to me that I didn't know; how could I not have? A year before my class had gone on a field trip to a museum where I became fascinated with a medieval chart showing how women contain minute individuals, all perfectly formed and lined up like so many sardines in a can, just below their navels. What's more, these individuals contained even more minute versions of themselves, who in turn held even more. Our fates were already perfectly mapped out within us, just as we once waited perfectly inside our mothers, who themselves were held within the depths of their mothers, our grandmothers. It's impossible not to revisit this twenty-year-old playground scene, wondering why I didn't go right when I should have gone left, or, alternatively, seeing my movements as inexorable and indefatigable. If the cancer was already there it would have been discovered eventually, though probably too late. Or, perhaps that knock set in motion a chain of physical events which created an opportunity for the cancer to grow which it might not otherwise have found. Sometimes it is as difficult to know what the past holds as it is to know the future, and it seems curious to me now, just as an answer to a riddle seems so obvious once it is revealed, that I passed through all those early moments with no idea of their weight.

2
Petting Zoo

A T FIRST THERE was only the presence of the boy beneath the bed to horrify me, but before I knew it his father was under there, and then, most shocking of all, even the doctor squatted down and tried his own ineffectual form of cajoling. This last bit of vaudeville was too much; not only were the doctor's assurances on par with some villain's comforting homilies, but it was all so . . . so . . . *undignified*. Personally, I was mortified. The boy, who was a year or two younger than me, wore red pyjamas with feet; his father was almost completely bald and wore thick glasses. He reminded me of a father-actor from a black-and-white TV show I watched in re-runs every afternoon after school. Partly I felt embarrassed on behalf of the father and the doctor, though I also maintained a degree of scorn towards them for indulging the boy's behaviour. But mostly I found myself deeply embarrassed for the boy. How could anyone sink so low as to hide beneath a bed? This went against every belief I held dear. One had to be good. One must never complain or struggle. One must never, under any circumstances, show fear and, prime directive over and above all, one must never, ever, cry. I was nothing if not harsh. Had I not found myself in this role of sick child, I would have made an equally good fascist or religious martyr. The subtleties of that very first visit to the emergency room, where I'd been praised as good for being brave, were already arranging themselves into a personal treatise the same way the most seemingly inconsequential archi-tectural miscalculation on the ground floor can result in a sweeping chasm in the penthouse. At a time when everything else in my family was unpredictable and dysfunctional – my mother had been discharged from a brief stay in a psychiatric hospital only weeks before — here I had been supplied with a formula of behaviour for gaining acceptance and, I believed, love. All I had to do was perform heroically and I could personally save my entire family.

At that point heroism was still fairly easy: I'd only been on Ward Ten in Babies' Hospital for about an hour. I wasn't happy about being associated with babies, but I was thrilled by the notion of being in the city, in a hospital that had twelve floors and an elevator. To this day I still find riding in an elevator a basically pleasing act, the progression of lights marking a sense of excited anticipation. Ward Ten was an old ward. Babies' Hospital was nothing like the shining clean techno-miracles I was used to on television and had experienced at the considerably newer Pascack Valley Hospital. The walls were a pale green and the floor was made up of darker green tiles speckled with grey, worn to an even darker green in those places where people made a habit of pacing throughout the years. All the doors were made of wood and the partitions, strategically placed for viewing purposes, were made of thick, sea-green glass reinforced with mesh wire. There were bars on all of the outside windows. Though the hospital was undeniably clean, a dingy air prevailed throughout. I was always a fan of the gleaming new, but in time I came to find this dinginess comforting, more humane than the fascinating but alien landscapes of newer wards I would later visit.

My name was called. Again, they called me Lucinda. Previously the name belonged only to the first day of school, but from that moment on I recognized it as the property of all people in uniforms standing in the unflattering, fluorescent light of hospitals. The doctor asked my parents a number of questions about my mother's pregnancy and my infancy, and sometimes they had to confer with each other in order to answer. I wasn't used to seeing my parents like this. I don't think I was used to seeing them defer to people in positions of authority; I don't think I was used to seeing them act together, pair up like this; and I don't think I was used to seeing them act so *normal*, like the parents of my friends in the neighbourhood, like parents I had seen on TV. It was generally assumed that we were not a normal family, a feeling we both proudly carried and tried to hide at the same time.

We, my parents, two older brothers, older sister and twin sister, had immigrated to America five years earlier, when Sarah and I were four. My father, a well-known television journalist in Ireland, had been offered a job he couldn't refuse with a major network in the States. He packed us all up and, in what was probably meant to be some sort of tongue-in-cheek joke about immigrants, had us all sail to America on a boat. Unlike our earlier countrymen who sailed in steerage, we travelled on the *Queen Mary*, on what was her penultimate voyage. Surely this grand act was to be the harbinger of the riches already awaiting us. As with most of my father's gestures, that voyage was well meant, but later, when things were not going quite as well, it was referred to with scorn, and, even later, after his early death, it seemed more an act filled with literary bathos, and pointedly sad.

Of course, at the time, it was all adventure extraordinaire, especially for a four-year-old gathering first memories. My brothers used to play ping-pong on a back deck and sometimes lose the ball over the side. I loved nothing better than to run and stare at its lostness in the churning water far below. The chaos held me tightly, endlessly. One day Sarah drank a glass of cream instead of milk and was sick all over the place, another time we were invited to a children's party in the gigantic ball room and I won a prize at Duck Duck Goose. In the ship's gym there was an electric horse, and a peculiar machine which involved a large strap that vigorously jiggled the fat-atoms in your bottom to smithereens. The most predictable memory of all, the Statue of Liberty, draws a complete blank, but I remember looking up and simultaneously hoping and fearing that the ship's mast would hit the Verazzano's bridge as we passed beneath it. New York, when we disembarked, was rainy and filled with broken windows.

'Where are we now?' Sarah and I asked our mother several days later in our new kitchen. She stood near the sink, her hair short and ash blonde and her shirt white silk. I was convinced my mother was the most beautiful woman in the world.

'We're in Spring Valley now.' She was patient with us.

'But when are we going to America?'

This struck her as funny. Her face lit up and I knew we'd pleased her, but exactly how escaped me. Spring Valley was just a name, a place, but America, now that was something big, a whole way of life, an idea, a piece of magic. Judging by the way everyone spoke of it all the time, I was eager to know exactly when we were going to be there.

My eldest brother Sean was seventeen when we left Dublin, my brother Nicholas a few years younger than him, and Suellen a few years younger than that. Sarah and I were only four and Dublin was just a collection of vague shadows to us. But for the rest of our siblings, Ireland was home and this new place to which they'd been unwillingly transported, America, could never match up. The virtues of Ireland and of England were constantly extolled. Many years later, when I moved away from the country I'd grown up in myself, I came to understand how small things such as certain brands of candy or particular television shows took on great symbolic meaning from that previous life. But these transformations of loss and symbol came much later. When we first arrived you could not eat so much as an American candy bar without being reminded by one of my brothers that it stood for the entire political and social inferiority of America. Sometimes, when a Crunchie, a British/Irish candy bar, would appear in the house – perhaps someone had mailed it – the feel of that orange wrapper in my hand seemed to conjure everything that I was missing. Television, I was also reminded, was vastly superior back in Ireland. I watched American shows and felt guilty for liking them, wondered why their counterparts across the ocean were so much more refined. I never doubted Ireland's superiority, I only assumed it was some failing of mine which prevented me from seeing it in precise terms.

My poor brothers, missing their home more than they could admit, felt nothing but contempt for this new one thrust upon them. The worst insults they could deliver became *That's so American*; *Don't be so American*; *How American*. If we were selfish or acted spoiled, we were *Becoming American*. When we used up all the hot water in the bath, that was an American thing to do. Gradually, my earliest memories of Ireland tranformed into pure myth. Where I was now was not only no good, but it was getting worse all the time. The flawless times of the family were past, I had missed them simply by being born too late. I began a lifelong affair with nostalgia, despite the fact I had only the vaguest notions of what I was being nostalgic for.

Apart from its vulgar culture, the worst aspect of America, according to my brothers, was its politics. They leaned towards the left back in Ireland, but in reaction to the conventional, Republican neighbourhood we moved to, in a country different in almost every way from the one they knew, they grew radical. Added to the list of insults along with American were Bourgeois and Capitalist; American-Bourgeois-Capitalist the most searing of all. I had no true idea of what these things meant, but I developed a healthy disdain for them, too. I remember my teacher in the third grade talking about some great and famous capitalist. It was during the first snow of the winter and she had a hard time keeping everyone from looking out the window except for me. I sat there tensely, wondering why she was describing this man with such admiration in her voice. I was waiting for the awful truth of what this Capitalist had done to be explained, but instead the teacher gave up and placated everyone by making snowflakes from coloured pieces of paper.

If I intuited that our family was different and in some ways superior, there were also obvious oddities about us not as easily defensible. Neighbours and schoolmates made fun of our different accents. Sean was, though I didn't understand this at the time, in the early stages of being diagnosed as a schizophrenic. Apart from that, he also had long hair and lived a 'hippy' life, much different from those of our neighbours' sons. My mother herself suffered from depression, an illness I also did not understand at the time. There were always money problems, even before my father became unemployed, and if nothing else, our home's drastic state of disrepair served as a reminder that there were things I had to keep from other people. So, to see my parents acting so much like, well, *parents*, other people's parents, there on Babies' Ten, surprised me, and momentarily even fooled me.

They spent the entire afternoon there with me, talking to doctors, talking to me, to each other. I met some of the other children, and their parents. I watched the drama of the boy in the red-footed pyjamas unfold as he was eventually extricated from beneath the bed, and how his mother held him in her lap the entire time the doctor did whatever it was he was doing to him. At one point I was sent down to Haematology for a blood test. I'd had several of these taken from my arm, but this was a finger stick. I watched the entire procedure, fascinated. When I stood up I couldn't understand why I heard a faint buzz and felt so light-headed. Afterwards I reported my dizziness to my mother, who simply remarked that I had been silly to watch. I was perplexed because I'd actually enjoyed watching the blood test and only now felt embarrassed by such a 'weakling' response. Ever since, I turn my head whenever someone approaches me with a needle.

I visited the radiology department for a chest x-ray. This department was newly renovated and, unlike the rest of the hospital, was painted in bright colours. It was the only floor which actually fitted my picture of a children's hospital. Murals of cartoonish animals and clowns stared merrily at me as I walked down the halls. In the waiting room I found an absurd number of half-broken toys and giant stuffed animals which sat dejected in the corners, too big and unwieldy to really play with. Being all of nine years old, I disassociated myself from all this baby stuff anyway, and made a point of looking disdainful and bored instead. I'd consciously packed no stuffed animals to bring to the hospital. It was of tantamount importance that I appear adult, strong, unafraid.

As the day wore on, as my parents stayed and met other parents, as I met other children and their parents, I began to believe that maybe, after all, my parents really were like these other parents, people I would have normally castigated for their indulgences, letting their worries and fears hang like pictures on a wall for everyone to see. Finally, as dinner time approached, the intern who'd examined me earlier explained to my parents (I listened in on him describing me in the third person), that he was going to do a bone marrow test on me. We were all standing in the hall together. Perhaps I was afraid of this test I'd never heard of, I can't remember, but when my parents said, 'Well, then, we'll be off,' I looked at them, panic-stricken, and asked, 'Aren't you going to stay with me?' They looked at each other, then back at me, and said something about the traffic, and besides, I wasn't scared, was I?

I felt my face flush. Things seemed to rush at me as if I were the focal point of some unseeable camera's close-up. I regretted everything, all my assumptions, immediately. The embarrassment I felt stays with me still, though of course it wasn't embarrassment.

That feeling was about as different from embarrassment as a patch of soil is from a tree, an egg case from a spider, a lump of stone from a sculpted hand lying heavily on an even stonier lap. It was the moment when I understood unequivocally: I was in this alone.

As it turned out, there really wasn't much to fear, not just then. The treatment room was small and overheated and possibly even cosy, a result of the room being too old for fluorescent lighting. The two interns who did the bone marrow test had only arrived on the ward that very day, the first of their rotation. I lay on my stomach on the stiff, clean-smelling white sheets covering the table, the night settling outside but the sky still velvety blue from the city lights. The interns seemed to have known each other from working together in the past, bent as they were on entertaining each other more than me, but I liked them instantly. I had no idea who this Mutt and Jeff team were, but they had a little routine down, switching into alternately squeaky and rough voices. They even thought it was funny when they pressed down on my numbed lower spine and my legs reflexively kicked the contents of the tray all over the floor. As it clattered on the green tile I tensed, waiting for the flare of anger I normally associated with even the most innocent of accidents, but instead they laughed at themselves, made jokes silly enough that we all groaned, awarded me ludicrously high numbers of points for being such a good sport, allowed me to feel at ease, at home even.

This sense of comfort continued in the following days and weeks. There were definite problems to face here, but to me they seemed entirely manageable: lie still when you're told, be brave. It didn't seem like so much to ask, really, considering what I got in return: attention, absence from school, occasional presents, and, though I wouldn't have admitted it to anyone even if I could have articulated it, freedom from the tensions at home. My father would stop by after work to say hello when he wasn't working too late, while my mother, who hated driving in the city, came in less frequently. Secretly, I enjoyed how some of the other visiting parents, the ones who came in every day, felt sorry for my lack of visitors and snuck me contraband food items. I played up to this expertly whenever I sensed a particularly orphan-sensitive audience. My mother would have been appalled if she'd known. I slipped in and out of my various personae with great ease, even flair. Being a child, my past was not yet a burden to me. It was merely there, and I felt a certain freedom which allowed me to suit the present to my needs, whatever might get me an inch somewhere.

I felt perfectly fine. Each day there would be one test scheduled, but more typically than not they consisted of various intricate scans and x-rays, which were relatively painless. I made friends with the other children, quickly discovering the hierarchy on that and all other wards. The truly sick were on the top of the hill, but of course being too sick worked against you as you couldn't enjoy the status. Anyone having an operation also ranked, though we always factored in how long your operation would take, how many you'd had before, and how gruesome the resultant scar would be. But the true deciding factor was seniority, how long you'd been on the ward, and in this, Derek was King.

Derek was a handsome boy with a serious dose of asthma and, I would find out much later, from an unstable home which inclined doctors to keep him in the hospital, with its warmth and wealth of, albeit bad, food, longer than was medically necessary. He had been in and out of the hospital many times already, and by the time I arrived he had a week or so under his belt. Despite his asthma he seemed to feel fine and the two of us together, relatively healthy and with far too much time on our hands, spelled trouble.

Afternoons were longest. Sunlight pushed its way in past the barred windows and bore down heavily onto the green floor like an algae infested lake. You could almost hear the bright overhead lights sigh when the nurses shut them off, and this was the moment Derek and I waited for each day, nap time when the ward was quiet and the nurses sat around their station, pretending not to care what we were up to as long as we didn't make any noise.

Sometimes the afternoons were planned for us. On another floor there was a playroom which boasted a large, ornate doll's house, a real collector's item probably donated by some well-meaning person. You could only look at it from behind its glass protection, but it was nice, too nice to be played with. It wasn't a doll's house but a doll's mansion with dozens of intricate, plush rooms filled with luxuries like tapestries and fluffy feather comforters on brass beds. There were perfect little spoons and forks, neatly made beds with teddy bears in the children's room, a bowl of milk in the pantry with Kitty stencilled on it. There were also old-fashioned items, possibly in use when the house was donated: washboards and iceboxes and chamber pots. This house had absolutely nothing to do with any of our lives. Most of the children in the hospital came from the surrounding poor neigh-bourhood, and this little house was nothing more than a rarified version of what they would never have and, with its protective glass partition, were not allowed to touch even in miniature. Sometimes you'd see someone standing there, staring, but for the most part the giant miniature house, despite its prominent position near the door, was ignored.

Every once in a while they showed a movie, usually just cartoons, in a lecture hall in another part of the hospital. Getting there was half the fun, walking through the main halls in our slippers and bathrobes, passing people in their street clothes. It was as if clothes spoke to each other, our childish pyjamas murmuring something special about us as we brushed past the suits and white coats and work clothes. The movie itself was usually awful, but Derek and I enjoyed making fun of it later, and guessing what was wrong with the other kids who filed in with us, pushing their various IV poles, holding specific parts of themselves delicately. Anyone who looked truly shocking, looked particularly ill or sported an impressive piece of machinery, was treated with respect. There was an implicit honour code: you never stared openly, you always did whatever you had to to help, you were always extraordinarily patient. Not that we weren't perfectly capable of being right little assholes, and indeed were in many other settings, but in the hospital, a kind of dignity reigned.

It was when nothing official was scheduled that Derek and I got up to our own tricks. At first we stayed on the ward, sneaking around in the storage room or whatever else place carried a forbidden air. Gradually, however, we took to sneaking out of the ward, where we risked getting caught by a dutiful nurse. The lobby was attractive for its gift shop. We stole get-well cards and gave them to other patients after signing them Love and Kisses, Michael Jackson. We thought this was hysterical. A few times we ventured down near Emergency. They had all the good magazines in the waiting room and there we lived in eternal hope that someone covered in blood would stagger in through the door, maybe even clutching a knife sticking out of their heart. It never happened. Over in post natal you could see minuscule 'preemies'. These hardly looked human, caged in their incubators like rare specimens on display, hooked up to all kinds of fascinating tubes and machines. It was a good thing they'd never remember any of it, we decided, and thought this lack of memory permitted us to ogle them in the painful and technological aftermaths of their precarious entrance into this world.

Though it seemed like an eternity, I probably spent only just over two weeks in the hospital. Every day I'd have some test and it never really even occurred to me to ask what was going on, what the tests were for, what the results were. At least, this is how I remember it, though my mother tells it differently. In my version, when the day came, the doctors took both my parents into my room alone. They stayed in there a long time. Finally, my mother emerged, explaining that I was going to have an operation on my jaw, but that I could come home for the weekend first.

I remember being thrilled as if I'd only heard the part about going home for a weekend. My mother looked at me aghast. She was acting strangely, I thought, not herself. I had to explain that it wasn't the operation I was excited about. I knew that if I went home for a weekend I'd get special treatment, and I did. My father let me go horseback riding not once, a big treat in itself, but twice. When my sister complained about the favouritism, my father virtually snapped, an uncharacteristic response but I was too excited by the proximity of horses, their sweet, grimy smell, to even try and figure it out. I don't remember going to visit my school at all.

In my mother's version, she comes out of my hospital room and remembers me jumping up, misunderstanding her. But after that, she says that the doctor wanted to speak to me, as if I were an adult. He told me I had a malignancy. He explained they would do everything they could, that I should do my best to get well and they would help. As my mother tells it I did go to school where I thanked my teachers and classmates for the cards they'd sent me. I told them that I had a malignancy. My mother said I seemed rather happy about it, that my teachers were rather shocked by my attitude. I told my teacher and all of my friends, probably with pride: I had a malignancy, I was going to have a *big* operation now.

Some time later, I don't remember exactly how much later, as my family was milling about the kitchen and I was leafing through the paper at the table, someone dated an event as something that had happened 'before Lucy had cancer'. Shocked, I looked up.

'I had cancer?'

'Of course you did, fool, what did you think you had?'

'I thought I had a Ewing's Sarcoma.'

'And what on earth do you think that is?'

My family seemed rather incredulous, but it was true. In all that time, not one person had ever said the word cancer to me, at least not in a way that registered as pertaining to me.

It was as if the earth was without form until those words were uttered, until those sounds took on decisions, themes, motifs. There may have been thousands, millions of words uttered before those incisive words, but these had no meaning, no left-over, tell-tale shapes to show they had ever, no matter how fleetingly, existed. I loved words, the sound of them. One of my favourite experiments was to pick a word, any word, and repeat it ceaselessly to myself until I was in awe of it, until it transformed itself entirely into an absurd sound, nothing at all to do with the thing it signified. Gull. Truck. Banana. Formula. And then, malignancy. I can reconstruct now that its important syllables probably charmed me; its promise of some kind of rare and dangerous implications made me feel important, but its lack of meaning provided me with just enough echo to act as background to my shock at hearing the word Cancer.

Lack of meaning had its own shape, it groped in the darkness, spoke to me only from a hole in the wall, late at night, when I dreamed of witches who apologized profusely before inserting their singing knives into me, explaining they were sorry, they didn't want to kill me but they had to, they were witches, it was their job. I never recognized these dreams as relative. I thought only of what was there in front of me like my experiments with words, shredding their meaning through repetition. My experiments seemed no more significant than my attempts to observe the moment when I fell asleep at night; watching in the dark like some prowler for that thin line between consciousness and unconsciousness.

I remember all the things I did with Derek very clearly and even nostalgically, going to the movies, peering through the glass at that dated doll's house, blowing up surgical gloves into mutant udders. Yet the random dreams, the casually forgotten words, point elsewhere, strike me as inelegant and incomplete. Language supplies us with ways to express ever subtler levels of meaning, but does that imply language *gives* meaning, or that it robs us of it when we are at a loss to name things? I can think of several interpretations to ascribe to a girl who doesn't remember invoking the word Malignancy, yet what do those theories have to do with me, who resists feeling anything other than bewilderment at the image of a child walking casually down a hall chanting agreeable, history-less words?

Sunday afternoons in the hospital were stillest, longest. Formless hours to be got through. All departments closed, there was none of the week's bustling; all of the familiar nurses were off, leaving you in the hands of unsympathetic aides who didn't care if you were entertained or not. In the stillness, the traffic on the street below emerged louder than before. There were more of other patients' visitors to watch, more obscure relatives who made the trip in from out of town bearing useless flowers and ornately wrapped toys. But I grew tired of scrutinizing them, grew to recognize the same swirling patterns and dynamics of every family that walked onto the ward complaining how hard it was to park around here, how long the elevators took. Some older brother or father would find a surgical mask and put it on and laugh, believing they were the first to discover this antic. I'd sit on my bed looking for words hidden in a jumble of letters, or vainly attempting to put together an incomplete jigsaw puzzle I'd found in the game room. The stiff sheets made the bottoms of my feet red, and I was always in trouble for not wearing my slippers when out of bed. A sweet smell drifted down the hall from the sluice room, where they cleaned the bedpans and kept the sterilizer.

I could always count on Derek, who would appear beside me when I most needed him, decked out in his blue bathrobe with Columbia Presbyterian spelled out in fading black letters across the chest. There was one particular Sunday we'd been waiting for all week. Several days earlier we'd overheard a conversation between two of the staff nurses and one of the residents, something about the building where they kept the animals. Eavesdropping on adult conversations was something I did automatically, but the word animals pricked at me.

'They have animals here?' I interrupted.

'A whole floor of them, over in one of the other buildings. They try out new drugs and operations on them, to help humans.'

I was very sensitive to being patronized and resented the tone with which this was said, but I was interested too.

'How do you get there?' The nurses and doctor were all young and good-looking. Though couched in jargon, their conversations often held overtones of flirting, their true meanings as clear to me as a shiny present, unseen by the intended receiver, held cumbersomely behind the besotted's back. I was probably annoying them.

'You have to go outside, across the street,' the young doctor said.

'Aren't there tunnels to it?' a nurse asked.

'I guess so, but I've never been down there, I'm not even sure how you get to them.' Then they were off again, talking to each other, ignoring me, but it was too late. This was the adventure I'd been waiting for all my life. As I took off to tell Derek, the doctors shouted back at me to walk. Just to annoy them, I stopped short suddenly and surfed a good three feet along the well-polished floor on my socks.

Our main problem was that we didn't know how to get to the tunnels. Finally, we were able to dupe a recently arrived teenaged Candy Striper into taking us, artfully making sure she didn't spill the beans to the nurses, who would have surely forbidden even the idea of such a thing. We convinced the Candy Striper that the nurses had said it was okay and, just our luck, she even knew where the animals labs were because she used to work there as a messenger. She fell for it so perfectly that she even invited two of the other children to come along. Sunday was the brilliant choice because none of the regular staff, who were always suspicious of us, would be on duty, and there was almost no chance of a doctor or technician coming to seek us out for some boring test.

This particular Sunday coincided with the first uncomfortably warm day of spring. All the windows were open but they offered no relief. My tee shirt clung to my back as I slipped off the bed.

Whenever possible I dressed in my street clothes. Wearing pyjamas during the day, despite the fact everyone else was wearing theirs, made me nervous and depressed. It brought to my mind the old practical joke where someone shows up in a chicken suit for a formal ball.

Once assembled in the hallway, Derek, the Candy Striper, the two other children and I headed for the elevators. I knew there was a basement beneath the ground floor, but I didn't know there were levels even beneath that. It was as if our bodies were transported through space to the very bottom, the terminus, SB2, sub-basement level 2. The doors opened on a long hallway with concrete walls, illuminated intermittently with bare lightbulbs cradled in bell-shaped cages of wire dangling from the ceiling. It smelled cold. You could see the imprints of the wood used as a mould for the concrete very clearly, as if you were looking at vast slabs of petrified wood.

Derek leaned over and whispered in my ear. 'This is where they keep the dead ones.'

The notion that at any moment we might see a white-sheeted body being rolled down the aisle made my fingers fall asleep. I shook them, bewildered by the effect. The Candy Striper walked forward authoritatively. But only fifty yards later, when faced with an intersection, she faltered. We scanned the walls for signs pointing towards the building where they housed the Animal Labs. For days I'd been looking forward to this. Once or twice a year a travelling Petting Zoo was set up inside the local mall. For a small fee you could walk around the sawdust-filled pen and pet the obese goats and sheep wandering around aimlessly. For an extra ten cents you could buy feed out of a converted bubblegum machine. I couldn't get enough of them, their smell, the clicks their cloven hooves made on the tile floor showing in patches through the sawdust. I was crazy for animals. Any book or television show or movie which had to do with animals I consumed greedily, though I shied away from ones where animals were over anthropomorphized. I thought it degraded them to be too closely aligned with the human species.

Uncharacteristically, Derek allowed me to walk in front of him. Normally there was a silent battle between us about who was in charge, but this morning he seemed distracted or, possibly, he just wasn't as excited as I was. There were things about Derek I didn't understand; he could get sullen like this sometimes. Though I would never have admitted it to him, I envied the fact he lived in the city year round. I thought it made him exotic. Once I awakened to him standing over me and two other boys peering in from the doorway: he'd kissed me. Perhaps they'd thought I'd be grossed out and wanted to watch, but my reaction obviously disappointed them. All I really felt was somewhat confused as to why Derek, who stood there looking equally confused, would want to do such a bizarre thing.

Eventually we found the correct tunnel which led to the correct building. We piled into the elevator and took it all the way up. The doors opened into a large foyer. Open windows with spectacular views of the city took up most of two walls. A cool, strong wind came in through them, and their unbarred expanses struck me as dangerous. Along with an unpainted ceiling and concrete floors, they gave the place a tenuous feel. One either side of the foyer were sets of swinging doors. We went arbitrarily through one set and down a hallway, realized it was wrong, turned back and went through the foyer again. As we opened the second set of doors the stink hit us head on. The tang of natural urea and ammonia mixed in equal parts with the chemical fumes of disinfectants burned the inside of my nose. This probably should have been an omen, but instead we continued on, down the hall, following the smell until at last we saw the doors: *Authorized Personnel Only*. There wasn't an authorized human in sight.

We pushed open the doors and found ourselves in a large room. Equipment of various sorts lined the walls and in the middle stood four interlocking pens with metal poles for sides. In two of the pens there were pigs and in the other two sheep. They had no bedding, and the concrete floor, dribbling with urine, sloped downward towards a system of grates. My first thought was how could they sleep on concrete? They'd been lying down previously but our entrance startled them. They stood up, the sheep bleating hoarsely and the pigs harumphing, very human sounding, and circled the tight interior of their pens. I'd never been so close to a pig before, and these were enormous. Pigs have human eyes, blue with round pupils. After staring at you they look away and you can see the whites of their eyes. Counter to every feeling I'd ever had about an animal before, I had no desire to go nearer.

We all just stood there in the doorway. Surely things were said, but I don't remember any conversation. As the sheep paced around I noticed parts of their fleece were shaved away into raw geometrics, framed for recently sutured incisions. One of the sheep had what looked like a plastic bag sewn into her side. We stepped back out and went into the next room: dogs had started barking. Half a dozen beagles in reasonably large cages greeted us joyously. One of the dogs looked unhappy and sick and ignored us, but the rest pushed with all their weight against their bars as we approached. As I neared the first one's cage, however, he stopped barking and growled at me. The Candy Striper heard and warned me not to get any closer to the dogs, most of whom looked desperate for attention. I hated her all of a sudden, her stupid outfit and shrill, silly voice.

Desperation saturated the room in those loud, whining cries pacing back and forth, back and forth, back and forth. I was overwhelmed. On each cage door was a sign with handwritten details about each dog, filled with alien words. Instead of water dishes they had hung bottles with tubes they could lick, giant versions of what my gerbils used, back home. Despite the warning, I let each of them lick my fingers through the bars.

The tenor of the expedition was shifting rapidly, it took on a slow, almost viscous quality. Our teenaged grown-up tried to hurry us along, now aware that she'd made a mistake. Opening the door to the next room we found walls lined with cages. The wall directly across from the door was filled with cages of white mice, and to our right as we walked in was an entire walls of cats, cage after cage stacked each upon the other. So many cats. I'd never seen so many cats in one place, and yet it was eerily silent. They crouched in their cages and stared at us, every single one of them, as we filed into the room. As we got closer some of them came up to the bars of their cages and rubbed, opening their mouths soundlessly. Years later I'd learn it is not uncommon to cut the vocal cords of laboratory cats, especially when you have a lot of them. They had the same water bottles and handwritten signs as the Beagles, but their cages were smaller. A number of the cats had matchbox size rectangles with electrical wires implanted into their skulls. The skin on their shaved scalps was crusty and red where it joined the metal. A lot of cats were tabbies.

It was too much now. There was a sound of monkeys in the next room, but we turned around and left. In the elevator, no one spoke, in the tunnels, no one spoke. A sad, groping presence accompanied us all the way back to the ward, where the lunch trays were just arriving and the aroma of spaghetti filled the halls. When asked where'd we been, our Candy Striper replied casually that we'd gone for a walk and not one of us said anything to the contrary. Sooner or later we all have to learn the words with which to name our own private losses, but just then we stood there, in front of the nurses' desk, speechless.

3

The Tao of Laugh-In

N O ONE CLEARLY explained just what was about to happen to me. Mary, the head nurse, did call me over to her at one point. Derek tagged along. The floors had just been polished and the lemon scent of wax filled the air. Mary was one of my favourite nurses, always kind and always the one most likely to crack a joke as she walked into your room with that dreaded basin, the one they carried needles in. Though I didn't mind blood tests, I'd developed a fear of pre-med injections, the ones they give you before taking you down to the operating room.

By now I'd had three operations, including a bone biopsy. Usually there were two injections, one for each thigh, and they hurt like bad leg cramps even minutes after they were over. Most nurses offered the hearty and useless advice of Rub that Spot Hard!, or, Squeeze your Toes!, but not Mary. She'd stand over you, needle poised, and announce her own joking version of comfort, mimicking that syrupy tone neophyte inflictors commonly resort to: *Now this isn't going to hurt me one little bit.*

I specifically asked Mary if she'd give me the pre-med for my fourth operation, the one which involved removing the tumour and no more than one third of the jaw. She seemed disappointed when she told me that she wouldn't be on duty for it. Late that afternoon, before she left, she called me over. 'This is a big operation you'll have tomorrow, you know that, don't you?'

I'd been told it would take a whole four hours, which was certain to elevate my social status on the ward. Though I'd felt sick after my other encounters with anaesthetics, I didn't comprehend what a four-hour surgery would mean. Somewhat chagrined at being spoken down to, I told her I understood everything perfectly, completely unaware that I hadn't a clue about how sick I was or what was going to happen.

She looked me right in the eye. 'Do you know you'll look different afterwards?'

For Derek's sake, I made a joke about bandages, about looking like The Mummy. Horror movies were a major source of entertainment for Derek and me. Between us we'd seen every bad monster movie ever made, and engaged in serious arguments as to whether or not Camera, a giant Japanese turtle, could win over Rodin, another Japanese creature with a somewhat pterodactyl look. Mary realized she wasn't getting anywhere with me. She shifted her weight, looked down and let her shoe slip halfway off her foot to dangle on the edge of her toes. After a few moments of contemplating this effect she put her weight back on the foot. I could hear the stockings rasp together on her thighs as she left.

The next afternoon, when I woke up in Recovery, I couldn't quite figure out where I was or what had happened to me. My entire body ached, and when I tried to speak, nothing happened. An elderly, overweight nurse approached my head from time to time with a long, clear plastic tube, which seemed to disappear just as a deep ache appeared in my lungs. I had no idea I had a tracheotomy. There was a loud, constant sound of machines, and at one point I amused the nurses, who showed me how to speak by placing a finger over the hole in my throat, by asking if they could turn them off so that I could get some decent sleep. My parents came in together for a minute, stood at the foot of the bed and considered me from what looked like a long, long way away.

With no room in Intensive Care, they decided to keep me overnight in Recovery. I held my hand over my throat, over my newest orifice, and felt my breath brush warm, almost hot, over the moist plane of my palm. The steady flutter didn't really seem to have anything to do with me. For the first few hours I vomited up large amounts of blood I'd swallowed during the procedure. I began to welcome the deep, lungy urge to release the sweet-tasting fluid from deep within me. It tasted almost pleasant. Drainage tubes drifted down onto the pillow beside me, the slightly shifting red and golden fluids of my body. An IV hung over me, dripping steadily and endlessly, a hypnotic effect similar to the spell of chaos I'd been drawn into off the stern of the boat which had brought me to this country. If I lay perfectly still, I felt no pain. I dozed and woke, dozed and woke all night, slept my half-sleep with an image of myself as swaddled.

Bizarrely, after they removed half my jaw, I limped. It was my first day up out of bed, I was going to traverse the entire four feet over to the bathroom. It required a certain amount of preparation, of disconnecting tubes and wires.

'Why are you limping? They didn't do anything to your legs, Chicken-chop.'

My mother was watching the nurse help me. I liked it when she called me Chicken-chop, the name she used with any of us when we were ill. I was back on Ward 10, with not only my own room, but my own full-time nurse. Most of the nurses simply sat beside my bed and read, but today there was one who liked to turn the television on without volume and chuckle at it continuously. Underdog was on the screen wavering behind my mother as she put down her knitting to view the spectacle of my first journey out of bed. I placed my finger over my throat.

'I don't know.'

It was everything I could do just to say those three words. My non-sequitur limping seemed to amuse both the nurse, my mother, and eventually me. None of us seemed to understand that the body is a connected thing.

Fluid was the major issue. I refused to drink enough. Or rather, that's how they perceived my inability to down more than a quarter of a glass at a time. Every swallow left me breathless, two swallows exhausted me, three and then four made me feel I should be congratulated, but instead they made an embarrassing chart and pinned it on the door, a magic-marker record of each and every cc I consumed. They thought the threats never to take out my IV would impel me, but they misjudged. I would have gladly spent the rest of my life on an IV if only they would just leave me alone.

Day after day passed and still I could barely manage a fraction of the ten glasses a day they wanted from me. Ten glasses! An unimaginable sum! Couldn't they see that? I knew that my mother was getting annoyed with me, beginning to take it personally. How could I explain that I really didn't want anything from them, that I just wanted to lie there, becoming ever more intimate with my body?

I knew all of my body's rhythms now, all of its quirks. The smell of my wound was sweet and ever-present, the skin on my elbows and heels as sore and red as holly berries. Though at first I'd dreaded the daily injections, now I didn't even mind them, welcomed the dozy contentedness they offered. I learned that all I had to do was relax, that fear was the worst part. I became a machine for disassembling fear. Even the worst pains could be rendered harmless if you only relaxed into them, didn't fight. I grew lazy about speaking, and even after I was given a full-time plug for my trachea, I put little effort into speaking, reducing my vocabulary to only syllables at a time, passing them out as cautiously as I did my attempts to drink only the most minute amounts of water. I grew weaker and weaker.

They started feeding me through a gastro-nasal tube, which had been inserted earlier. Each meal time a tray arrived with my name on it, a tray filled with liquidated *everything*, even turkey. I asked them to let me smell each container before they poured it into the tube. Aroma alone started to revive me. I could feel the hot or cold of the liquid pass through my nose, the back of my throat. Finally, at about five in the morning of my tenth birthday, I tricked a nurse into giving me some orange jello. It was the first thing I'd eaten in a week, and instantly I felt better, began to see that this bed wasn't a continuous state, that one day, one way or another, I would feel better.

When my whole family came to visit me for my birthday, I sat in a wheelchair and gazed at them, feeling splendid. I could tell they were shocked by the sight of me. I had been an absolutely normal nine-year-old last time they saw me, only ten or so days before. My older sister spoke politely to me, as did my twin sister. They'd never been polite to me before, and I knew that a chasm had opened up between us; how could I ever explain that how I felt now was actually *better*? How could they ever know where I had just come from? Suddenly I understood the term: Visiting. I was in one place, they were in another, and they had come only to pause. We made polite conversation about people at school, from the neighbourhood, talked about things entirely inconsequential because it wasn't the subject which counted but the gesture of conversation itself. You could have parsed each sentence not into nouns and verbs but into signs and symbols, artificial reports from a buffer zone none of us really owned, nor cared to inhabit.

My mother was the Visitor Extraordinaire. She'd arrive each afternoon, give me whatever bit of news or information about my health she had as quickly and simply as possible, then sit down in a chair and begin knitting. From beginning to end, she'd spend the entire visit knitting. Human presence is the important part of visiting, she understood that. Her body occupied a space close to my body, but it didn't aśk anything of it. Other visitors were more awkward, casual friends of the family who'd stop by and stand over me for long and clumsy minutes, trying to engage me in conversations, when really all I wanted was for them to sit down, relax, not say a word.

My father was the worst visitor. He loved puns and would think of a more terrible one each day. But what was wrong with his visiting was the awkward silence that followed his rehearsed routine. What should he do then. Sometimes he'd put on a surgical mask and make a joke about Dr Dad, exactly the same joke I'd seen dozens of other fathers make with their kids. Then he'd sit down, bereft of a vector, and stare intently at the drip of my IV. He could sit there like that for a long time, personally coaxing each drop of water to form and fall. I knew how hard it was for him, he probably knew how hard it was for me.

There were certain afternoons throughout that first big operation and in later years when I could recognize my father's particular gait far down the hall. He'd come to see me on his lunch break, though he didn't have much time to visit me with his work schedule being so hectic. We both knew that his visits were slow and sorrowful for both of us, and that it was okay that he could only come occasionally. One day I heard his step echoing towards me. Carefully, still not entirely sure of what I was intending, I got into my bed and closed my eyes. His loud breathing and hard-soled shoes entered the room. Silence stood over me for a minute or two, contemplating. I heard hands and coat pockets fumble around for a minute, the crinkle of paper, a pen covering it with soft thips of sound. Then at once everything was leaving the room, pulling out of it and leaving behind that specific, hollow sound of emptiness. I opened my eyes and read the note I found on my night table. 'Lucy, I was here but you were sound asleep. I didn't want to wake you. Love, Daddy.' I felt I'd let us both off the hook, yet still, after that, the afternoon seemed long and interminable, something to be got through.

Gradually, I began to improve. I gained strength, the various tubes began to disappear, and walking became less and less of a heroic effort. I still resisted speaking, however, keeping my answers down to a simple yes or no, and even then only when I could not nod my head. I allowed people to believe it was difficult, though my mother knew better and kept at me constantly. One day Mary came in when I was alone and announced very casually that I was much better now, that someone else needed this room and that, because there were no beds on this ward, I was to be transferred to the floor above. She left as casually as she had come. It was the first day I'd got dressed in regular clothes, into a Spiderman shirt someone had brought as a present. A feeling of regret came over me. Perhaps if I'd not got dressed they would still think I was sick enough to stay. A few minutes later an aide came in to help me pack. I excused myself and went into the bathroom, where I was overcome by weeping, the first tears I'd shed since I'd been in the hospital.

How could they just throw me out like this? I had come to believe the nurses there liked me, that they were my special friends, yet now I was just being tossed away. Only then did I begin to realize how accustomed I'd grown to being taken care of. I hadn't even had to wash myself. And as much as I hated to concede any points to my mother, I knew I had become too passive. An ornate and manifold surge of grief came over me, too complex for me to know what I was grieving for. Luckily, I tired easily and the weeping could only go on for a matter of small moments. I wiped my eyes. Ashamed of myself, I went back into the room to help the aide gather my things into a red plastic disposal bag with WARNING: HAZARDOUS WASTE written in large black letters across it. My mother had taken my overnight case home early on because it took up too much room.

The new ward was laid out exactly like Ward Ten, but all of the faces were different. It was filled with a different kind of patient

44

too, a group of teenaged girls who giggled with each other and told jokes about the doctors that I didn't get, especially one Dr Silverman, whom they all seemed to be in love with. One girl with long black hair and lovely dark eyes sang his name over and over again in a voice I told her was good enough to be on the radio. She looked pleased when I told her this. All of them were skeletally thin and, knowing nothing of anorexia, I wondered what was wrong with them. There were no visible scars or signs of illness that I could see, apart from their weight. One of them was so thin she couldn't walk and the others pushed her about in a wheelchair. Her arms were so thin that her elbows looked like giant swollen lumps, her hands like the oversized hands of someone who has worked long and hard their entire life. Though they were older than me, having already entered that mysterious, enviable realm of teenager, they wore toddler-sized name bands, the only ones small enough to fit their delicate and fragile wrists.

A week passed on the new ward, but I never committed to making friends there. Derek came up to see me once or twice, but then he too was finally discharged. My body started orientating itself towards home, feeling stronger and more bored every day. I still had sticky circles on my chest, remnants of the ECG, and my fingertips were covered with small black marks, scars from the daily blood tests, but my body was my own once more. I had looked at the scar running down the side of my still swollen face, but it hadn't occurred to me to scrutinize how I *looked*. Though I was now missing a section of my jaw, the extreme swelling which stayed with me for two months hid the defect. I hadn't really had much sense of what I looked like previously anyway. Proud of my tomboy heritage, I'd dogmatically scorned any attempts to look 'pretty' or girlish. A classmate named Karen had once told me I was beautiful, and by the third grade two boys had already asked me to be their girlfriend, requests and comments which bewildered me. When Derek delivered my first actual kiss only ten or so days earlier, his desire had taken me completely by surprise. On the day I finally went home I felt only proud of my new, dramatic scar and was eager to show it off.

School was already out. The endlessness of summer stretched out before me, sweet and narcotic. I wasn't allowed to go swimming because the scar on my trachea was still soft and fresh, a pink button on my throat, but I didn't really mind. I was a hero. Neighbours stopped me on the heat-rippled sidewalks to ask me how I was. Evan, my closest friend from the neighbourhood, and the other boys seemed suitably impressed with my hospital tales (I embellished heartily) and with my coup; I didn't have to make up any of the two months of school work I'd missed.

One afternoon when Evan and I were playing an intricate game of jungle in his living room, his father passed through on his way to the kitchen. Pausing in the doorway for a moment, he turned around and addressed me directly. I knew that his wife had died of cancer several years before, but I couldn't have imagined what went through his mind now to see a child with the same disease, the same prospects. He was the first person to bring up chemo and looked at me steadily and sadly for a minute before asking if I knew what it was. I'd been told I was going to have chemotherapy, but it had been described simply as another drug, another injection, maybe one that would make me a little flushed, but no more. I'd had some unpleasant scans involving injected dyes which had transformed the world into something woozy and hot, but nothing I didn't feel I couldn't face again.

My explanation didn't really seem to be what he was expecting, but, either unable or unwilling to finish what he'd started, he mentioned something vague about chemical changes in my body, about how my hair might be affected. Having no idea what he was talking about and sensing something serious I'd rather not pursue, I made a joke to Evan about how my hair would turn green, my eyes purple. This was the second time an adult had tried to approach me directly and seriously about my situation, and it was the second time I turned it around, refused to tackle it.

Death had become part of my vocabulary when I was six. The gerbil was the latest in a long line of family pets to die, and I was with my sister Susie, who was twelve at the time, disposing of the body behind the house. Our dog Cassie had died a year or so before and though I missed her, at the time I felt confused by Susie's irrational tears ands bad tempers in the days afterwards. Now the gerbil was also dead and though I'd had no real attachment to him, I was sorry. He lay on top of a brown paper bag from the A&P, soon to be his final shroud. His fur parted and clumped together in an unusual way, the deadest thing about him, and when I touched him I couldn't believe how hard, how cold, he was. Susie picked him up by his tail, the sunlight suddenly coming out and illuminating the dullness of his still open eyes. A strange idea entered my head, an idea surely so preposterous it couldn't be true. How could it be? Surely Susie would laugh at me for even suggesting it, but I felt I had to make sure anyway, for my own peace of mind.

I paused for a moment, considering how best to phrase it. I went for the negative approach.

'People don't die, do they?'

She looked at me with the surprise I'd hoped for, the faintly amused look which told me my fear was unfounded, but her response became proof positive that one should never ask a twelve-year-old sister *anything*. With glee in her voice she commenced to describe in great detail the cold dark ground you went into, how the skin fell off your bones, how your eyes fell out and, in a truly inspired touch, she began singing:

'The worms crawl in, the worms crawl out,
  in your stomach and out your mouth.'

I don't blame her. I was an easy mark and had I been in her position I'd have done exactly the same thing. Part of the job of being human is consistently to underestimate our effect on other people, and for the specific job of being a twelve-year-old with a younger sister, cruelty is *de rigueur*. She had no idea, as we stood there outside the driveway, what had just been implanted in the deepest part of me. No one had any idea, not my parents or teachers or friends, because there was no way I could even discuss it. If the word death was even mentioned in my presence, I would literally collapse. At night I dreamed of being carted off and left alone in a dark, cold room filled with bones, bones which would wake up once I was in there and dance around me.

There was a small dark hole in the steps in front of our house which led nowhere in particular, it was simply a structural defect, but in my new dreams it became the gateway to a world which terrified me, a world where people had no heads, or, if they did, they were filled with worms and beetles. This was what awaited me, there was no way I was going to escape death, and as the days passed I became more and more frantic. If I saw a movie or television show which involved someone's death, I'd hide under the covers. When a schoolmate I didn't even know died tragically in a fire, I was convinced that I was somehow responsible.

Why had we been born if this was the terrible end we had to look forward to? My six-year-old self was privately obsessed with my terrors and questions when salvation appeared in the most surprising of places: the television show 'Laugh-In'. A repeating skit, mixed in between all the sexual and political innuendos that were over my head, involved the scenario of a ragged, exhausted man climbing to the top of a large mountain. At the peak sat a man with a long, grey beard. Once the climber had reached the guru, he would ask straight out, 'Oh master, what is the meaning of life?' Of course the answer was always a silly one, usually resulting in the climber's falling off the mountain, yet I'd seen references to a similar mountain and guru in the cartoon 'BC'. Then I saw a National Geographic episode which located this mountain with its guru in an actual place called Tibet. Immediately, I went to my father. He was sitting in the living room, reading on the red couch so accustomed to his body that it obligingly swayed to hold him more comfortably. After his death I used to curl up into this space, lie there with the cats, the warmth of his physical dent as reassuring as some ghostly hand in my hair.

'Daddy, how much would a plane ticket to Tibet cost?' I asked, offering no explanation for my question.

His eyes went up into his head and he scrunched up his forehead, to let me know he was thinking. Looking down at his palm, he pretended to do calculations, muttering to himself. After a minute of this he turned and looked at me as he would an adult. 'One million dollars,' he announced, as seriously as I had asked him. I thanked him and left. Being six, one million dollars was about as unintelligible a sum as one hundred, but I decided to start saving. I understood it might take some time, possibly years.

Gradually, the obsession with death was replaced with other obsessions, with new, daily discoveries about what it meant to be alive. But for a long time after I put myself to sleep at night by imagining the mountain, the long arduous climb. Each step I took was counted off the way other people counted sheep, and each night that I actually made it to the top I'd ask my question, yearning to hear every minute vibration of sound, believing that the simple act of perfecting my ability to listen was all I needed to know the answer. Truth was something that existed, it's just that it lived far away.

I had long forgotten the trauma of the gerbil when I became ill, and the idea that death had anything to do with me directly didn't even enter my mind. It wasn't so much a matter of avoidance, but the simple belief that nothing bad would ever, could ever, happen to me. Sometimes I wonder if it wasn't this disbelief which kept me alive. Not even later, when it was unavoidably obvious to me that I was very ill, did it ever occur to me that what was happening was important, dangerous. Despite a knowledge of death, it never rationally occurred to me that I might personally be implicated.

As a teenager I worked in a library and one day, as I was reshelving books and bored, I found myself in the medical section where a book on paediatric oncology caught my eye. Pulling the heavy thing out, I laid it on the table, opened to the index and looked up my cancer, Ewing Sarcoma. I turned to the given page and read a brief description of the various manifestations of it, followed by a table of percentages, mortality rates. A reasonable chance of survival was given at 5 per cent.

The paper of the book was heavy and almost cream in colour, and I ran my finger along the letters which were so black I half expected to feel them raised up on the page. I looked up. The room was empty and buzzing both with bad light and the numerous stacks of books I still had to shelve. *Five per cent.* I felt obliged to say something, but no one was there and I didn't know what I was supposed to say anyway. Placing my hand on my neck, feeling my pulse there, I stood for some minutes on the verge of either moving or speaking or sitting or *something*. But I couldn't think of what it was, and then it passed over, I was on the other side of it, feeling like there was something I'd forgotten, some name or object or emotion I'd meant to take note of but had carelessly allowed to slip by. Finally someone walked into the room, breaking the silence with their winter boots squeaking on the floor, and I turned, reaching for another book to shelve.

4
Fear Itself

THE ROADS IN New York city are their own country. A knowledge of them gives one a sense of power. It makes no difference that, for the most part, New York is a giant grid, ludicrously traversable when compared with such labyrinths as Paris or London. Its power heaves up from the pavement right in front of your eyes, steam escapes in fits and starts as if the whole place were going to blow up any minute, people who have already blown apart lie crumpled in its crevasses, and all the while there is a thin promise, a slight wheedling tone, that something important, something drastic, is about to break.

I drove with my mother into the city five days a week, every week, for two years for the radiation treatment, and then once a week for another half year, to finish out the chemotherapy, which was administered most Fridays, with periodic 'vacations' over the two and a half years. My mother worked mornings in a local nursing home, and came to pick me up at our house at midday. We got into the car in our suburb, drove for just under an hour through the relative countryside of the Palisades Parkway, propelled ourselves across the Hudson via the George Washington Bridge and found ourselves deposited smack in the middle of another world. Billboards advertised the good life in Spanish, ancient cobblestones still showed up in patches through the tar, tar which shivered and smelled in summer and shone black and cruel in the winter. Grotesque figures loomed everywhere, but they didn't frighten me, nor did the filthy and the slobbering insane, the homeless and the drunk. What terrified me was the great expanses, the chasmic spaces between all of us, the distances none of us seemed prepared, or willing, to reach across.

I felt it keenly and, in truth, it didn't always seem like such a bad thing.

Even as I was spooked, I was impressed and admiring of the constant chord of toughness and strength which acted to harmonize all the many and varied notes in the city, the thousand and one little vignettes of overheard conversations, glimpsed-at lives. I didn't so much see any of this distance as recognize it. My mother and I usually drove the miles to the city engulfed by our own private, inner travels, the radio filling the front seat like an anaesthetic, and once we got to the city and went through the customary parking ordeal, we walked the few blocks to the hospital in silence. This was the routine we fell into, it seemed natural to both of us.

The radiotherapy department existed in a specially built section deep in the guts of the hospital with cement walls many feet thick. Chris, my 'radiotherapist', explained it was careful regulations that made the walls so thick. She placed her hand on the otherwise innocuous, pale yellow plaster and told me in reverent tones about the care one had to take around radiation. She herself wore a thick green smock made of lead. She let me hold it once, even though it seemed to weigh as much as I did.

On my first visit I could tell Chris was keen for me to see her 'as a friend'. Her hair was streaked blonde and her arms were strong and athletic. Her uniform was in an unbecoming yellow which clashed against the yellow on the walls. The entire department had a different feel from the rest of the hospital, offset by a cocoon quality and genuine attempts to make something human of this lead and cement hole in the ground. The employees here hung up family photos on the reception area walls, and if they didn't have their own kids yet, they put up overly cute pictures of cats and dogs. Posters of orang-utans proclaiming *Every time I figure out the rules, they change them*, and puppies thanking God it was Friday adorned the ceilings of the treatment rooms, demanding attention as I lay on my back.

Radiation treatment itself was a breeze, about as complicated as an x-ray. I'd get up on the table, Chris would don her lead smock, and turn out the lights. Bulbs from inside the clunky machine hanging from tracks on the ceiling would shine down on my face, waiting to be aligned with the magic-marker x's drawn onto my neck and face earlier. 'Hold your breath!' the command would come from somewhere in the corner, and I'd inhale as deeply as I could, almost always thinking about a movie I'd seen, a maritime disaster in which the hero had to swim a long distance underwater in order to save everyone else. I'd held my breath along with him, wondering if I too had it in me to save the others. Believing that one should be prepared for any emergency, I went about trying to improve my breath-holding capacity, and lying there on the gurney in the radiotherapy department seemed as good a place as any to practise for a disaster at sea. As the machines over my head clicked and whirred softly above, my body swelled with air, trembled almost imperceptibly with the desire to let it all fall away from me, deflate back out to the place it had come from, and just when I was about to abandon all hope and let the salty water fill my lungs, Chris's voice would sound from the dark corner.

'Breathe!' The overhead lights came on, Chris appeared without her lead burden, helped me off the table and it was all over again until the next day.

If it was Monday, Tuesday, Wednesday or Thursday, then that was the whole procedure. I'd find my mother in the waiting room, then we'd take the long elevator ride back up to street level, get back in the car and head home, hoping to avoid rush hour traffic. Friday was different. Every Friday, usually around three o'clock, was my appointment with Dr Woolf at the chemotherapy clinic.

I was already two weeks into the radiation treatment before I had my first appointment with Dr Woolf, and despite the early warning attempts of Evan's father, I went into it completely unprepared. Radiation, at that point, seemed like a sweet deal, all that time off from school, no pain, or at least not yet, the meditative drives into the city with my mother. The only thing that really worried me about chemo was the prospect of weekly injections, because that's all I thought it would be, an injection. If I had been blind to what the original operation would be like, and blind to warnings about this, once I entered the clinic I began to get my first intimations of what was about to commence.

In sharp contrast to the new radiotherapy department, the chemotherapy clinic was old looking, drab. The main waiting area was on one side of a much used hall, a main thoroughfare for the hospital. It was completely open, like a lounge, and on the walls hung dark oil-paint portraits of men I either never bothered to learn the names of or can no longer remember. The couches and chairs were covered in a dark green vinyl, the floor was black tile with white traces almost worn out of existence. The fact she couldn't smoke drove my mother insane, especially since week after week for two and a half years, we had to wait at least two hours past our scheduled time before my name was called.

The other people in the waiting room fascinated me. We all looked exhausted. The relative health of the people there seemed to vary widely, and over the years I became expert at diagnosing what sort of drugs children were receiving from their appearance. Some of them looked bloated and sluggish, others were thin as rakes, and almost everyone was in some stage of either losing or growing out their hair. Hats, scarves and even wigs prevailed. That first visit I felt apart from the rest of them, felt a million miles away.

Once we were finally in Dr Woolf's office, my mother ready to scream from the long wait, we encountered his telephone, apparently a permanent appendage. He could carry on a conversation with my mother, me, his nurse, his secretary down the hall and whoever it was on the phone simultaneously; he had it down to an art. My mother thought him incredibly rude, and she was right, there was nothing personal about Dr Woolf. His manner was gruff and unempathetic. The first time he examined me I could only flinch at how roughly he handled me, his large fingers pressing hard into my abdomen, prising open my still stiff mouth. His appearance didn't help. Tall, large-featured and balding, he had a peculiar, large white spot on his forehead which caught the light in an unflattering, sinister way. His nose was tremendous, his lips invisible. He scared me.

His office was as drab as the waiting room, but saved in the end by a large, multi-paned window which looked out onto a well-tended courtyard with banks of blue flowers and ivy-clenched trees. I spent a lot of time looking out of that window. I spent a lot of time forcing myself to look out of that window, because even on that first visit I knew that the inside of this room was no place for me, that the only thing I wanted to know about this particular interior was its implicit exterior, an existence that had nothing to do with me, Dr Woolf, my mother, the treatment table which was too tall for me to get onto by myself, or the two sixty-cc syringes waiting patiently in their sterile packets.

This first time examination was more thorough than the ones I would later receive. I was asked to strip down to my underwear, which I did, feeling humiliated and exposed. While he talked to the nurse, my mother, and on the phone, which was tucked beneath his chin, he prodded me with his free hands, hitting me just slightly too hard with his reflex hammer, and speaking far too loudly. When he touched me I could feel the vibrations of his voice in my own chest, feel them lapsing through my body's cavity the same way you feel a car passing too closely. He got out a tourniquet and wound it tightly around my arm, pinching the skin just like an Indian Burn you'd receive on the playground and, despite every ounce of strength I could muster, I began to cry. Not loudly, not even particularly heartily, just a simple dose of tears which, it turned out, were as accurate and prophetic as any I'd ever shed.

The butterfly needle, named for the wing-like holds which fanned out from its short, delicate body-like cylinder, slipped into my arm, a slender pinch I barely felt. Because it was inserted into the crook of my arm, I had to sit there with my arm rigidly straight, holding it up awkwardly and overly self-consciously. I began to grow warm, a caustic ache began settling into my elbow. For a split second, it was almost pleasurable, a glowing, fleshy sense of my body recognizing itself as a body, a thing in the world. But immediately it was too much, I felt the lining of my stomach arc out and pull spastically back into itself like some colourful, disturbed sea anenome.

It was an anatomy lesson. I had never known it was possible to *feel* your organs, feel them the way you feel your tongue in your mouth, or your teeth. My stomach outlined itself for me, my intestines, my liver, parts of me I didn't know the names of, began heating up, trembling with their own warmth, creating friction and space by rubbing against the viscera, the muscles of my stomach, my back, my lungs. I wanted to collapse, to fall back onto the table or, better yet, go headfirst down onto the cold floor, but I couldn't. The injection had only just begun, this syringe was only halfway empty and there was still a second one to go. My head began to hurt. Not sure if my brain felt like it was shrinking or swelling, I squinted around the office, not in the least bit surprised to see a yellow-green aura surrounding everyone, everything, like some macabre religious painting.

My body wanted to turn itself inside out, wave after wave of pitiful attempt to rid itself of this unseeable intruder, this overwhelming and noxious poison. I shook with heaves so strong they felt more like convulsions. Someone lifted a metal basin to my face and I quickly deposited everything my digestive system owned into it, and when that wasn't enough I came up with the digestive juices themselves, pitiful spoonfuls of green bile, and when there was no more I just simply threw up air, breathing it down in deep gasps between buckling it back up with spasms that ached with their own fruitlessness. It was the emptiness that hurt the most. When my stomach had something to offer back it was happy to do so, but when the convulsions ran out it still came, pressing inward with even greater self-spite, punishing its own lack by squeezing ever harder.

Gradually, the waves of vomiting subsided, leaving behind an unacted upon nausea which seemed to involve not just my stomach but everything, even my feet, my scalp. As a result of the vomiting my sinuses swelled and ached, but knowing nothing about sinuses I could only report that my nose hurt. Dr Woolf looked puzzled by this, but didn't follow it up with any further questioning. Someone helped me put my clothes back on; I don't remember the walk back to the car.

The sky was so blue it was almost transparent, and it moved seamlessly outside the window as I lay in the back seat. The trip home was simple, right from the bridge onto the parkway, off the parkway, down a few streets and then up the driveway. Though it was a half-hour trip I calculated only nine actual turns from start to finish. Not used to this vantage point, without the normal visual landmarks, I stared at the sky and attempted to guess where we were, and each time the car turned I tried to visualize exactly what it was turning towards: Exit 14, the supermarket, the stone house on the corner, our house. Somewhere along the line I messed up. I thought we were at least two more turns away but suddenly I felt the rise of the driveway and knew I was wrong, but it would be the last time. Over the years I perfected the mental drive, could do it even when I was half asleep, even when the rhythm was interrupted by a sudden need to vomit into the kitchen mixing bowl my mother placed on the floor.

That very first time I arrived home I remember not feeling quite so bad. Somewhere along the way home I'd begun to feel less nauseous, or at least better able to control it. My father suggested I eat something, some ice cream perhaps. My head swimming, I sat at the kitchen table and ate several spoonfuls, my parents looking at me expectantly.

'It wasn't so bad, was it now, Lucinda Mag?' my father asked.

I nodded my head no, purposefully bringing another spoonful of the vanilla, chocolate and strawberry mixture up to my mouth. Speaking seemed like something one could grow tired of.

My stomach rebelled. I stood up quickly and made my way over to the sink, where I threw up the now liquid ice cream, still cool and even soothing as it made its way up. For some reason, I started to cry. My mother put her hand on my head and tried to soothe me, and when I was done began to explain that there was no need to cry, that everything would be alright, that I mustn't cry.

How could she ever know I would take her so seriously? She went on to explain how disappointed she was that I'd cried even before Dr Woolf had put the needle into me, that crying was only because of fear, that I shouldn't be afraid, it would be alright. It was one thing to cry afterwards, because she knew that it hurt, but why did I cry beforehand, hadn't I always been so brave before?

I looked out of the kitchen window over the sink I had just thrown up into. Straggles of spiderplant cuttings had taken over most of it, the brown, tangled roots filling an assortment of drinking glasses placed on the ledges. There was also a collection of small ceramic houses, presents and mementos accumulated over the years. Immediately outside, overgrown and sloppy fir trees presented their own tangled view, preventing any clear angle of the front lawn or street.

Sometimes the briefest moments capture us, force us to take them in and demand that we live the rest of our lives in reference to them. What did my mother mean? Part of me knew then, and still knows now, that she was afraid for me. If somehow she could convince me not to be afraid, we could rally around the truism she had grown up with: there was nothing to fear but fear itself. My mother didn't know how to conquer *what* I was afraid of, nor could she even begin to tell me how to do it for myself. Instead, out of her own fear, she offered her own philosophy, which meant in this instance that I should conquer the fear by not crying. It was one sentence out of her, a fleeting thought she probably did not mean, but for me, who would have done anything to find a way out of this pain, this brief statement she doesn't even remember making would be one I'd never forget, and as I made my way downstairs to my room, I resolved never to cry again.

I kept my bedroom dark, only letting the light from my television change colour on the wall beside me. Every hour or so I felt a great urge to lean over and retch into the mixing bowl on the floor. I drank water constantly simply so as to have something to throw up. As soon as the vomiting was over I'd feel whole continents better, and what had been unendurable only moments before, the intense nausea, was suddenly bearable, exposed as a fake, something I'd only mistakenly thought I could not bear a second longer. I'd lie back on the pillow feeling both energized and exhausted at the same moment, and, gradually, over the next hour, the feeling of unbearableness would return, subtly, insidiously, until I again had to lift myself up and hang over the side of the bed, my intimate bowl beneath me. This went on all night.

The second day was better, the cycle of turnover between nausea and relief would gradually extend, so that I was only throwing up every four hours, every six hours, only three times during the night. The third day was breaking point. I could actually eat something, something innocuous like tapioca. I'd quickly learn to judge food not by what it tasted like in eating, but how it tasted when I threw it back. Vanilla pudding was best, though it turned an unfortunate colour, making me opt for chocolate for purely aesthetic reasons. I'd try to leave it down long enough so that I could digest most, possibly even all of it, before my stomach rebelled yet again.

Sometime during the late afternoon, relief would come. A flicker at first, only a moment, but for that brief moment I understood I was going to get better, that this was going to end. I sat up in bed, felt the strength of my body support me. Another moment would go by and I'd feel ill again, my head beginning to throb, but an hour, maybe two hours later, the feeling would return, stay for just a few breaths longer before abandoning me, then a period of illness followed, returning just a few shades briefer, and so it would go on, through the evening. When I woke up on the fourth day I felt only a little weak, a little washed out, but glorious and high, that sanguine, comfortable feeling one gets after performing some great physical feat. I had swum the Channel. I had climbed Mount Eiger.

I sat up, listening for the sounds of my mother's footsteps, the clicking of the dog's nails on the tiled floor. A tree obscured my window, shattering the light into patches on the dirty glass. I didn't understand how I could have overlooked the sheer joy of these things for so long, how the intricate message of their simplicity had escaped me until just this moment. This weightless now-ness, this ecstasy could sometimes last me all day, at least until that afternoon, when it was time to go back to the hospital for the radiation treatment, which, as I've said before, didn't seem so bad, not really, anyway.

The fifth day was Tuesday, my favourite day of all. All but completely recovered, yet relieved from the burden of school, I was free to wander about the still house, form intimate relationships with the cats and dogs who regarded me non-judgementally as I tracked their movements over the living-room floor, sleepily following the inexorable arc of the sun. Tuesday was still far away from Friday. It was futureless, thoughtless, anxiety free.

The house itself mothered me. With everyone else away at school or at work, I somehow thought my eavesdropping created a new meaning for the clock, or the hot water heater, the cats growling over their food, that my listening made for them, and for myself, a real home. The house empty was a different place from the house when occupied.

With so many brothers and sisters, I'd never experienced such opportunities for privacy. I liked to go into my mother's closet and sit there in the dark for the sheer pleasure of smelling her while at the same time knowing how annoyed she'd be if she knew I'd invaded her privacy. I became a snoop, going through everyone's drawers, looking for things that might give me clues to how other people lived their lives. I liked to go and lie on my sister's bed, look out of her window, think to myself, *so this is what she sees when she wakes up in the morning*. What was it like to be somebody else? I went into my father's bedroom, dark and cluttered, and saw all the bits of paper, the stray ties, the dirty cups, as marks of how little he was touched by his personal surroundings, how little they, in return, touched him. It all seemed so random to me, so accidental. In my brother's room I found magazines with pictures of naked women, fascinating me for reasons I couldn't determine. His room seemed the most alien of all. Even when I lay down on his bed and saw what he saw, I knew I wasn't even close.

The long, elliptical mornings of invading other people's privacy while alone in the house seemed endless, but eventually I'd hear the car drive up to the house and know it was time to leave for the city. Except for Fridays I looked forward to the drive, counting gophers serenely eating grass along the highway, seemingly unaware of the danger only feet away from them. I also pretended that I was riding alongside the road with a great, graceful swiftness on top of a large, black, gleaming horse, its sensual mane tangling with my face, the rhythm of its hooves a hypnotic lecture on how to arrive someplace entirely different.

Indefatigably, Friday, or D-day as we began calling it, would commence its approach. Wednesday held anxiety at arm's length, but it was still there, just on the edges, and I knew it. Thursday was almost unbearable. Friday morning I woke up, early as always, but did not want to get out of bed, even to go and lie on the floor with my best friends, the dogs, who I imagined understood my suffering, thinking that their wet tongues licking my face weren't random or casual, but pointed, intended, rife with sympathy.

The second week of chemo was worse in that I knew what to expect. This presented a curious reversal of fear for me, because I already understood that with most other types of pain the fear of not knowing about it usually brought about more suffering than the thing itself. This was different. This was dread. It wasn't some unknown black thing hovering and threatening in the shadows; it had already revealed itself to me and, knowing that I knew I couldn't escape, took its time in the stalking. This was everything I ever needed to know about Fate.

We went through the whole routine all over again, the endless waiting, Dr Woolf's eternal phone call, his strong hands on my body. I tried not to look at the syringes beside me, but when I looked out of the window Dr Woolf invariably passed in front of my line of vision, casually holding a syringe in the air. When I looked down at the floor, I somehow chanced to look at the exact time and in the exact spot where Dr Woolf sent a brief spurt of fluid out of the syringe in order to clear air bubbles out of the needle. An otherwise graceful and thin arc of liquid fell directly onto the tile I was concentrating on. I took it as a sign to cry, which I did, ashamed of myself, unable to meet the eyes of my mother, who began telling me not to, to hold it back. The tourniquet went on and it began all over again, just like last week, except this time when I got home I went straight to bed, I didn't even try to sit up, to eat anything as grotesque as ice cream. I felt my mother was disappointed with me. I hadn't gone straight to bed last time, why was I doing it this time? She came to my room and sat at the edge of my bed. She looked tired, but beautiful, always beautiful to me, her make-up exact and perfect, the redness of her lips, the faint hue of her powder, the distinct, sweet smell of her perfume.

'You can't let this get you down, you know. I know it's hard, but you can't get depressed by it. Don't give in to it. You were not so bad last time, so make sure that what you're feeling isn't just in your head.'

She sat there a moment longer, staring at me sadly, before asking if there was anything else. When I said no she stood up and left me, alone with the television. My father had rigged up a buzzer that ran up to the kitchen which I could press if I needed anything. For the first few weeks I pressed it every single time I threw up, but as time passed and I failed, as I saw it, to not vomit too much, I began leaving the vomit in the bowl, even when it smelt awful, and only buzzed when the large vessel was full. I lay there in my room the way one might lie alone in the forest at night, dimly sensing something large breathing close by, and feeling the eyes of something unfathomably lurid turning upon me.

My father bought me toys not because he believed even for a second that they would sufficiently compensate me, but because it was about as close a gesture as he could manage. He didn't really have the stomach for the treatments and only on the rare days when my mother was ill or otherwise busy would he take me in for the chemotherapy. His rhythm was entirely different from my mother's. We arrived late, so there was not as much waiting time, though he seemed happy to sit there for as long as he could reading his paper. Once my name was called he'd accompany me into the office and exchange greetings with Dr Woolf, but as soon as I was asked to take off my clothes he'd turn to me and say, 'Right then, I'll go and get the car.' Perhaps in part he was embarrassed to see his daughter half naked, but I knew that he did not want to see me suffer.

He'd jangle the keys at me, just as he did with the dogs, for whom the level of excitement at that familiar sound approached heart attacks. He'd smile and announce, 'I'll be right back,' adding in explanation, 'this way you won't have to walk so far when it's over. I'll double park right outside and come in to get you.'

I watched his back as he left and felt relief, because his embarrassment and awkwardness caused me just as much pain as they did him. There was no blame in those moments, no regrets, no accusations, not even despair. Those things came later, when I learned to scrutinize and judge the past, but at the moment his leaving was a great enabler. Knowing that my father had his own burdens, his own failings, allowed me to continue on through what would otherwise have been unbearable. As an adult, I wonder how could he have left me alone in there, but as a child I knew the answer to this clearly, and knew that as soon as he was out of the room I was, if nothing else, free to respond as *I* chose. My father's nervous whistling of Bobby Sherman's 'Julie, Julie, do you love me?' faded down the hall as Dr Woolf turned to me with his tourniquet and I turned to him with my unfettered grief.

My moment of truth with my father was brief, followed mercifully by privacy and a sense of relief. It was harder to maintain such a sense of transcendence during the appointments with my mother. She stayed in the room and still, despite my repeated failures, insisted that I not cry. Although one summer day, it must have been summer because we were all hot and red-faced, I remember my mother bending beside me. The needle was in my arm and I was feeling the first hot flushes in my stomach. I could smell her perfume, stronger than normal because of the heat. 'Don't cry,' she was whispering to me, as if it were a secret we were sharing. Dr Woolf's voice was resonating over both our heads, talking to neither one of us. Perhaps it was something in her voice that day, maybe it was the way everything shone and vibrated with the heat, but for the first time in a long while I lifted my eyes up from the still empty basin and looked at her. Her own eyes were filling with water, tears that would never fall but hovered there, only inches from my own.

Suddenly, the way I perceived the world shifted. I wasn't the only person in the world who suffered. I had always heard the cries of other children who wailed from behind closed doors all along the corridor just outside Dr Woolf's door, so it would be false to say that I found myself hearing them for the first time or more clearly. What happened was more hallucinatory than that. My sense of space and self lengthened and transformed, extended itself out through the door and down the corridor, while at the same time staying present with me, with my mother, who, to my profound discovery, was suffering not just because of, but also for me.

Moments never repeat themselves exactly. Simply because I understood something important and urgent and graceful there on the examination table, looking at my mother's blue, red-rimmed eyes, didn't mean that only seconds later I wasn't back in another moment in which I hated myself for crying, for not being strong enough. The beautifully simple revelation I had with my father in Dr Woolf's office was followed by his parting, his footfalls dimming down the hall, leaving me alone to contemplate what I had just learned. My mother's very presence forced me to be present, disallowing me to dwell in the moment, and the comfort I gained from understanding her pain was both fleeting and insidious. Fleeting because such is the nature of all moments, and insidious because once I had tasted of the freedom and transcendence of my epiphany, I wanted nothing else but to return to it. I confused that graceful state of mind with the attached solace and comfort it brought, so that when the next injection came, the next bout of crying, and I *wasn't* able to not suffer I felt I had only myself to blame, felt that I had failed in some unknowable, spiritual way. In my mind, I didn't have what it took: I didn't deserve to be comforted. At night I dreamed that the children I was baby-sitting for had drowned, slipped down to the bottom of the pool we had been standing by. Try and try as I might, I could never fill my lungs with enough air to reach the bottom where they lay struggling, the eerie light lapping over them and, afterwards, their useless corpses rising up to the surface. I had to go to their parents, my empty arms outstretched towards them, my clothes soaking wet, and explain what had happened, how I had tried my best, really I had, but still, it wasn't enough.

5
Life On Earth

Next to the garage was a small island of grass, surrounded by a sea of driveway asphalt on one side and a front-walk of cement on the other. Smack in the middle a meagre fir tree splayed its boughs just high enough from the ground for me to sit in the shade beneath them, the earth dark and sweet smelling. To the south I was able to survey what amounted to my version of a grassy plain, and to the north, a jungle of thick moss which grew up around the mouth of a gutter pipe. This was my kingdom. Plastic animals bought at the local drugstore inhabited it and together we lived our urgent lives.

The lion, my favourite, had muscles permanently rippled into his hard plastic body. He lived in the cave I built for him out of stones not far from the gutter pipe. Every morning I took him out of the fresh grass bed I'd made the previous night, and together we surveyed the island, checking on the other animals safely tucked into their own domiciles. The aardvark was stashed beneath the tree, the ibex and giraffe installed on the border of the grassy plain, the zebra roamed between the jungle and the plain, and the snake I delegated to the rocks near the tip of the island. Manufactured by a different company, the snake's size and colouring made him slightly incompatible with the other animals and as a result he never quite received my complete care. The animals never came inside the house, never left the island, which as far as I was concerned was the most authentic aspect of their lives.

My mother insisted that I wasn't taking very good care of them when I complained that one of the dogs had chewed on my giraffe or zebra during the night. How could I explain why it was crucial for me, safe inside my bed at night, to think of them out there, living their continuous lives regardless of my presence? I especially loved the nights when the weather picked up, imagining my animals braving the elements, the wind and rain relentlessly beating down. Every morning I had the distinct sense that I was simply opening the door on an ongoing world, one which continued into the growing dark or while I was stuck inside, too sick to get out of bed. My imaginary world simply carried on, constant and sure.

When I wasn't on my island, I was riding for the Pony Express, though sometimes I was a Martian, sent to this planet on a surveillance mission. I was myself only in the briefest of moments, the most passing of encounters, a stranger walking brusquely by in the hall. As an alien, I could transform myself anywhere, anytime. Sometimes I was still a human, but one sent here from a future so distant there was no way I could comprehend what the everyday things of the present time meant, while other times I was an alien who'd taken on human form, walking imperceptibly amongst a race mistaking me for one of their own. I'd sit in the car, or in waiting rooms, and examine everything around me carefully, objectively. What exactly was this peculiar ritual of the toll booth? What was the significance of the different types of footwear? The whole trick was to forget myself, forget what I really knew, break all my preconceptions.

The only time I was ever completely myself was on Fridays. There was no way to escape the pain. Yet with each successive week the visits to Dr Woolf's examining were less and less about physical pain. The shame and guilt I felt each week were attached to what I viewed as my failure not to suffer, which began to grow unbearable. The physical side seemed almost easy in comparison. Was this how my body dealt with the onslaught, veering the focus away from itself, insisting that its burden be lessened by having my mind take on more than its fair share? Whatever it was, it worked. Worked in the sense that I became adept at handling my pain, deft at addressing its various complaints and demands for attention.

I'd lie in my bed and concentrate on letting the tremors run their course, allow them free access to all of me so that, like some bear sniffing me out, they'd gradually grow bored and slowly amble away, leaving me alone and exhausted but still alive. Some pain, like the pain of a needle or the site of an operation, is specific: it announces itself in no uncertain terms. Often I tried to balance the pain out with the rest of my body, a sort of negotiation where I'd isolate one section. I'd lie there and list to myself the parts that didn't hurt, trying to feel them, aware that normally I'd never have any reason to 'feel' my body or know it so intimately. Vaguely, I was becoming aware that I was experiencing my body, and the world, differently from other people. For hours I'd lie either in my bed at home or in the hospital, running my finger back and forth along the wall or bedrails beside me, conversing silently with myself in the third person, rationalizing the situation, setting down the basic premises of my secret philosophy, occasionally even telling myself I was lucky, lucky to have this opportunity to know such things. At times, I was desperate and could find no solace anywhere, nothing seemed to work and the weight of being trapped in my own body made it difficult to lift even a hand off the sheets. Other times, a sort of physical awareness would take hold of me. Each breath was an important exchange with the world around me, each sensation on my skin a tender brush from a reality so beautiful and so mysterious that I would sometimes find myself literally squealing with the delight of being alive.

It was when the pain centred around my head that it was the most difficult to deal with. It's one thing to ignore your arm or your stomach, but ignoring your head isn't quite so simple. The radiation treatment was beginning to take its toll and open sores began appearing all over the inside of my cheeks. The first time I felt them was while eating a bowl of tomato soup. Each mouthful stung and, never having been told that radiation burns were an expected side effect, I suspected the soup of being no good. When I thought no one was looking, I carried my bowl from the living room where I was eating in front of the television and into the bathroom where I overturned it into the toilet. The soup sunk in scarlet, silty swirls to the bottom of the white porcelain and I let it lie there for a few moments before flushing it away. I didn't want to say anything to my mother because I was afraid she'd see this as yet another of my ploys to not eat. I was losing weight rapidly and all anyone ever seemed to do was shove food in my face, food I had little interest in. Eating had become a monumental effort and I was at a loss as to how to explain to my mother or the nurses that simply eating one boiled egg was tantamount to an act of heroism.

Now there was this new element to add to the already long list of why it was hard for me to eat: not only did I have trouble chewing and swallowing, not only was my stomach in turmoil half the time, but now it actually *hurt* to put food in my mouth. It went from bad to worse. As the radiation treatment went on it got so that I could eat only the blandest of foods. Any sort of fruit was out of the question – drinking orange juice felt as if I was rinsing my mouth out with battery acid. Anything salty, or even as vaguely spicy as ketchup ignited my tongue and the raw, tender skin of my cheeks. I lived almost exclusively on oatmeal, disgusting protein drinks that practically had to be forced down my throat, and endless dozens of junk-food chocolate cream rolls, my mother's welcome bribe for the protein drinks. I loved eating entire boxes of these disgustingly sweet and fatty things slowly and with embellished delight in front of Susie and Sarah, who were both eternally on some new diet.

After every six series of weekly injections I was admitted to the hospital, to my beloved Babies' 10, for a five-day course of intensive treatment. I actually looked forward to these times in the hospital: the doctors set up the IV and administered the yellow fluid slowly and continuously. These didn't make me feel as intensely ill as during the weekly injections of a concentrated dose, but even if I did feel ill, so what? I simply threw up in my basin and lay back in my white bed, secure in the fact that there was no one around who cared too much one way or the other if I threw up or not, cried or not: I felt free and sovereign. I was considered a 'regular customer' on the ward. I knew all of the nurses, knew the routines and jargon and often I found myself explaining things to the rookie doctors who rotated on and off the ward. With no school responsibilities to speak of, no family tensions to deal with, I considered going into the hospital something just short of a vacation.

Even now, hospitals elicit intense nostalgia in me. That vague longing, which attaches itself to almost any version of the past, as if context and not content are what really count. A feeling rises up in me and though I know for a fact I was often in pain, I remember myself as being happy there, lying in the heavily starched sheets, the sound and movements of other people just outside the door.

At home, it was different. Those long quiet mornings in the

house still gave me pleasure, but as soon as that silence was broken, as soon as anyone entered the front door, tension and shame accompanied them. Unable to locate my unhappiness as within the difficult and complex family relationships we all shared, I thought all of it originated with me, that I was somehow at fault. If I couldn't overcome my growing depression, I deserved it, and how unfair of me to inflict it upon everyone else, upon my mother especially.

I was willing to do absolutely anything to get out of the weekly chemo shots. There was only one way to do this, and this was to be too sick to withstand it. Holding the thermometer up to the lightbulb's heat and other elementary school tricks were ancient history. I had to *really* be sick, have a measurable increase in my white blood cell count to indicate an infection.

My first experiment in making myself ill came about innocently. It was early winter, everyone was asleep except my father, who was working late again. Icy rain was falling all over the state. News reports warned people not to drive if they could avoid it. The temperature was hovering just at thirty-two degrees. The local television station showed a map of New York with cotton ball clouds floating over it, clouds weeping blue rain drops mixed with white circles of hail. The whole picture looked like the thought-balloons over cartoon characters' heads, as if New York state itself was *considering* icy rain, thinking it over. It was Thursday.

I lay in bed thinking about my island, and suddenly I was overcome with a desire to go outside and see my animals in the storm, see how they were braving the elements. I thought of the real cows I'd seen from the car standing staunchly in their fields, shivering, the black part of their hides gleaming wetly, a faint steam rising up off them. I got out of bed and pulled down my long flannel nightgown, which had bunched up around my waist in bed. Without bothering to put on shoes, I walked towards the garage door and let myself outside as quietly as possible, trying not to waken the dogs. I felt the chill run up my legs.

My animals were fine, just where I'd left them. I was disappointed that the rain only shellacked their bodies instead of being absorbed into them in dark, shiny streaks, like real skin and hair would allow. Standing there, only a few feet from the door leading back inside, I began to shiver. That's when it hit me. If I stayed out here, I was going to catch cold. I was going to get sick, perhaps even sick enough to raise my white blood cell count. It seemed like the perfect plan. Walking into the dark back yard, I found a spot where I knew that no one looking from inside the house would be able to see me, and lay down on the cold wet grass. I tried looking up at the black chalky sky, but the rain kept splashing into my eyes, forcing me to close them. How long would I have to stay out here? What would I do with the evidence of my wet nightgown; if I hung it near the heater, would it dry before my mother saw it in the morning? The cold began to get painful. My teeth chattered. If I couldn't stay out here long enough, if the discomfort of the cold drove me inside before I had a chance to get really ill, would that mean I was a failure even in this?

My nightgown soaked through, making it almost transparent. I could see my tiny nipples, pink and hard, and below them, the edge of my sharp hips sticking up. I lay there until I couldn't stand it anymore, until my fingers were stiff and red and starting to swell. Once inside again, I pulled off my nightgown and hung it over a chair. If my mother found it, I would tell her I'd thrown up on it and washed it myself in the sink. It was sensual and delicious to be back in my warm bed, the sheets absorbing the water of my naked skin. I fell asleep almost instantly, a rarity for me.

But the next morning, I felt fine. I woke up and saw the wrinkled nightgown still on the chair and remembered what had happened. I breathed in deep, expecting to hear soft rales in my lungs, but there was nothing, not the slightest hint of congestion. Sitting up, I tried to gauge how I felt. Did I have a fever? Was my throat sore, did I feel weak at all? No. I felt perfectly fine. I didn't even feel tired. In fact, I felt better than I had all week, which seemed like the cruellest joke, seeing how it was Friday, and in only twelve hours I would be right back in this same bed, throwing up.

I sought out different ways of getting sick. I experimented with drinking dishwashing liquid, but all that did was make me *feel* ill without actually *being* ill. I was too scared to try any other poisons I could find under the sink, having met two boys in the hospital who didn't have lips or tongues or even throats, these having been burned away from drinking things they themselves had found beneath the sink. Roy, the one boy I was friends with, had a feeding tube in his nose which he swung about like an elephant's trunk. Charlie, the other mouthless boy, was younger and had a mean look in his eye; whenever I was admitted to the ward I scanned the chart list for his name, hoping he wasn't there.

My pet project was inhaling water. Once before while nauseous, I'd inhaled some of my own vomit causing my lungs to react instantly with a case of pneumonia. Unfortunately for me, the pneumonia came at the very end of a cycle of shots, right before Christmas, which they were planning to get me off for anyway. If I could somehow get a small amount of fluid into my lungs, I figured I'd be set. I filled the bathtub, and, on the count of three, submerged my head. Breathe, I'd tell myself, breathe. I saw it as a battle of my own will. I saw it as a test of *forcing* myself. Normally I'd lie there until I ran out of breath, re-emerge for some more air, then sink back under again, firmly telling myself that this time, I was going to do it. When I finally found it in myself to open my mouth under water after countless attempts, my body would automatically heave itself up, sputtering water. For a moment my mouth and maybe even my throat filled with water, but the violent coughing I couldn't suppress prevented the water from reaching my lungs where it counted. The water sloshed in the bathtub around me and even over the sides, displaced by my violent actions. And the white towels, soaked from mopping up the water on the floor, hung like flags of surrender over the bathtub.

Most drastically, I experimented with scratching my arms with rusty nails I found lying on the street. A case of tetanus, the lockjaw everyone thought I'd had in the very beginning, still seemed like a preferable deal in comparison to chemo. I remember sitting on the stone steps one afternoon in our back yard, the summer sun glaring down. I was listening to the screams of the neighbourhood children I hardly ever played with any more, trying to scratch myself with the top of a dirty tin can. Again, something held me back, and while I could get a good welt up, I never scratched forcefully enough to break the skin or draw blood. Something always held me back, and for the longest time, I thought it was cowardice.

Letters from strangers all across the country started arriving for me in the mail. Somewhere, somehow, my name had found its way onto a Catholic prayer list. Coloured stationery bordered with flowers, cats, intricate motifs. Inside, the letters were usually short, written in rounded, elongated hands. All of them assured me that Jesus loved me, that if I loved him he would take on his share of the burden. One woman sent me a picture taken from her kitchen window, a snowy backyard with a bird feeder covered with sparrows. 'When I'm sad,' she told me, 'I look at my birds, and they make me happy.' Letter after letter confessed similar thoughts, advised me to think happy things, think of kittens, of foods I liked to eat. My entire family got a kick out of reading these letters. We mocked them out loud, laughing at the naivety, the unbounded simplicity of these letters with our bitter, cynical air. Every letter promised a prayer said in my name.

I laughed along with my brothers and sisters, but part of me longed for the world of those letters, the same way I longed for the world I watched on television, on 'Father Knows Best' and 'The Brady Bunch'. I fantasized about these shows, imagining what would happen if one of their children got cancer. Everything would be talked about, everything dealt with. No one would ever lose their temper. No one would go unnoticed.

Along with the letters came pamphlets, Christian publications mostly geared towards children. They told stories of mysterious strangers who appeared on the doorsteps of troubled families, strangers with a special shine to them, a kind look and a light in their eyes. A quality of calmness and fairness infused the difficult tasks the stranger performed, whether he was mediating in an argument between the parents or helping an invalid. He virtually glowed with love and peace and understanding. It was as palpable as a physical feature and everyone who met him could not help but notice. After a few days he left the family, having impressed upon them how they too could be as happy and peaceful if only they let God into their lives.

In the secrecy of my room, I decided I wanted this Light, this peace, this glow. Except that the scenarios always ended the same, leaving the troubled family to ponder and resolve to change. I always wanted to turn the page, wanted to know how or what the troubled family could actually *do* in order to believe? After all, I was sold, I wanted to have Jesus help me out and make me good and strong and pure, all of the things I was sure I wasn't, but exactly *how* was I supposed to go about doing this?

Sooner or later we're all driven to this same point. In secrecy, away from my family and our shared scorn over the cards and their simplistic sentiments, I sat myself down in my bedroom, on its blue carpet, and I asked, 'God, if you exist, prove it to me.'

What was I expecting? A voice, a verbal affirmation? A physical one? I looked down at the carpet I was sitting on: I half expected it to change colour. A sudden light, maybe? I looked up into the air above my head for it. I knew I only half expected an answer. Was my partial belief preventing God from speaking to me? Didn't I have to *fully* believe, or did all this simply mean that there *was* no answer? I hugged my knees close into my chest and rocked back and forth on my heels. I couldn't bear to think I was wrong, that somehow everything I was going through didn't actually mean something.

I stretched my arm out in front of me and flexed it, opened and closed my fingers, the tips of them covered with small black dots from the continuous blood tests' lancets. I resolved to Believe, even in the face of this lack of response. Was it possible to prove my worthiness by repeatedly asking the question, even in the brunt of this painful silence? In the same way I was sure I could prove my love, and lovability, to my mother by showing her I could 'take it', I considered the idea that this was what God wanted from me as well, to keep trying and trying and trying, no matter how difficult it was. My goal, and my intended reward, was to understand.

Life became more complicated at home when my father lost his job at ABC, where he worked in the news department. With the loss of his job came the loss of his medical coverage. Luckily my mother's job was able to take up part of my coverage, but we were still in a bit of a bind. Things became more tense. Days were filled with phone calls and letters and endless forms to be filled out. Nights were filled with even more arguments about money. The hospital pharmacy, which had been covered on my father's plan, sent the drugs used in my treatment up to the clinic. Now, we had to pick up the drugs ourselves and pay for them up front. To my extreme horror, this meant we had to store them in the refrigerator at home. Every time I opened its door there they were, a row of short glass vials lined up in the butter rack. The way the cold light glinted off them made my stomach lurch.

For some inexplicable reason, the new coverage, which was so inadequate in so many ways, paid for an ambulance to transport me to the hospital each day. The notion thrilled me. But the day the ambulance actually pulled up in front of our house made me feel self-conscious and awkward as I walked down the lawn. A group of neighbours had come out to see what was happening and stood there in a circle, watching. 'I'm not really that sick,' I wanted to tell them, 'this is just a big joke, get it?' Despite the fact I knew I'd lost weight and was a bit pale, I never actually did consider myself all that sick. I already considered myself separate from them because of what I'd gone through, but it didn't occur to me until then that people might actually *pity* me. The idea appalled me.

As horrified as I was by the idea that people might view me as someone to feel sorry for, I also knew that I possessed a certain power. After all, people noticed me. Wherever I went, even just to the store with my mother, I was never overlooked. I could count on at least some sort of attention, and I discovered that people were embarrassed when I caught them looking at me. I stared right back at these strangers with my big blue eyes, which appeared even bigger now that I'd lost weight and that the right side of my face was starting to sink in without a bone there to shape it. They always looked away as quickly as possible, trying to pretend they hadn't been staring at me at all.

If this type of attention wasn't always comfortable for me, it nonetheless further defined me. Most people struggle all their lives to avoid fading unnoticed into the crowd, but this was never my concern. I was special. Being different was my cross to bear, but being aware of it was my compensation. I knew for a fact that when I was younger, before I'd got sick, I'd wanted to be special, to be different. Did this then make me the creator of my own situation?

The ambulance rides continued for only a few short weeks, until my father got a new job at CBS and I was again covered by his medical insurance, meaning no ambulance and no more storing the drugs in the refrigerator. I was relieved on both counts. My mother and I took up our own daily drives to the hospital once more. The whole way there I stared out of the window and imagined myself on a horse, galloping on the strip of grass alongside the road, jumping the irrigation ditches and road signs. The horse was black and I could feel his mane in my face, his dark hair warmed by the sun warming my own hands and legs, the rhythm of his stride constant and sure, comforting, going someplace.

6

Door Number Two

EARLY ON IN the treatment my hair began to fall out. While I had been warned, I was taken by surprise the first day I reached up to sweep my hair back and a handful of my long blonde hair came out in my hand. I guess I'd never really believed this would happen. I was sitting in the car with my mother when I first noticed it, and I started to cry. At a loss to say anything that would be able truly to comfort me or stop my hair from falling out, my mother reminded me that I did know this would happen, that I shouldn't get so upset, as if foreknowledge of an event could somehow buffer you from its reverberations. Feeling, again, that I had failed simply because I was upset made me cry only harder.

My hair had never been something I'd thought much about. Compliments were paid to me because of it, but these sorts of things had never particularly interested me. I can remember several occasions when people had told me or my parents that I was pretty, but I would have considered acknowledging such a thing myself as too 'girlie'. More often than not, my hair seemed like a bother to me, something which got in the way while wrestling or climbing trees. But now? When I undressed at night, I heard the static of my sweater as I pulled it over my head, then saw the long strands on the collar waving in the breeze of its electricity. I'd sit up in bed in the morning and look down at the tangled strands on my pillow. As water ran out of the bath, I had to sit on the edge of the tub and reach over several times in order to free up the drain. Once an aggressive, careless brusher, I now patted at my head with a comb very carefully and very gently.

Involved as I was with the physical process of losing my hair, I somehow ignored the appearance aspect of it. I knew that I was going bald, I knew I was pale and painfully thin, and I knew I had a big scar on my face. In short, I knew I was different looking and I knew my appearance had an effect on other people which I could sometimes use to my advantage. But I was still keeping myself ignorant of the actual details of my appearance, of the specific logic involved with it. My intuition must have known it was better this way.

In the same way that I understood the extent of my illness, while not actually admitting I was ill, I spent a very long time not acknowledging I was going bald, even as I swept my own hair off the dog's black coat after a particularly vigorous hug. I was too young, only ten, almost eleven, to be any Samson. Sex appeal was relegated to toothpaste commercials, while sex itself was still a mysterious thing, clues to which could be found in the pages of my brother's magazines. Though mysteriously compelling, I mostly found these slightly repulsive and regarded sex, whatever it was, as something which I'd surely never take part in. I looked at myself in the mirror with a preoccupied pre-adolescent view, which is to say that I looked at myself, but I didn't judge myself. When the first taunts and teases were thrown my way, usually by some strange kids in the supermarket parking lot, more often than not I was able to come back with an insult far more sarcastic and biting than their own rather unimaginative Baldy, or Dog Girl. I understood that their comments were meant to impress each other more than actually harm me. I possessed a strong sense of self, and lived vividly in my world of hospitals and animals and fantasy. I had no sense of myself in relation to many of the people around me, the 'normal' people I walked by every day. I was naturally adept at protecting myself from the hurt of their insults, and felt a vague superiority to them, for the moment, anyway.

Sometimes in the hospital days or even a week would pass before I was well enough to get up and wash my hair. I hated the way it got oily and lanky and bunched up into tangles behind my head from lying on it so long. That first morning I could get up and wash it was always a great relief, but there finally came the morning I asked my mother to help me wash it and she looked at me sorrowfully and suggested, in a sweet voice, 'Maybe it's time to cut it.' And that's what we did. She borrowed a pair of scissors from the nurse's desk and while I sat in a chair she snipped off what remained of my hair, my white, white scalp shining through. We discovered, for the first time, that I had a large birthmark on my head, over my left ear. The next morning she came in with a hat, a small white sailor's hat, which I put on and almost never took off for the next two and a half years, even during the cyclic periods when my hair was growing back out. Sometimes it grew several inches and was perfectly presentable as hair, but I knew it was only going to fall back out and I refused to be seen in public without my hat. My hat. It became part of me, an inseparable element of who I thought I was.

My hat was my barrier between me, and what I was vaguely becoming aware of as ugly about me, and the world. It hid me, hid my secret, though badly, and when people made fun of me or stared at me I assumed it was only because they could guess what was beneath my hat. It didn't occur to me that the whole picture itself, even with the hat, was ugly, and as long as I had it on, I was safe. Once, while watching television, I saw someone lose their hat in the wind and I immediately panicked for them, for their sudden exposure. It was a visceral reaction. And as the teasing continued, both from strangers and from the very boys who I'd once regarded as friends, I began to suspect that something was wrong. I identified the problem as my baldness, as this *thing* which wasn't really me, but some digression from me, some outside force beyond my control. Yet, even while I identified this problem as separate from myself, I assumed that once the problem was solved, once my hair grew back out, I would be complete again, whole, and all of this would be over, like a bad dream. I still saw everything as fixable.

During this time my mother was still working in the Occupational Therapy department of an Hasidic nursing home, and most of my mother's co-workers were themselves Hasids. Hasidic law dictates that once a woman is married she must cover her hair. This used to be done with kerchiefs, but now the most common method is to use wigs. I imagine that these women grew tired of their wigs the same way other women grow tired of their clothes, because there seemed to be a surplus of discarded wigs in the community. As my mother's friends became aware of my predicament, they generously began to donate these hand-me-down hairpieces. My mother didn't know how to refuse them, and the first time she came home with one we all had a good time in the kitchen playing with it, trying it on ourselves first and then on the cats. When I put it on I looked as ridiculous as my brothers and sisters, not to mention the cats, and so it was all a big safe joke. But more wigs kept coming home with her, sometimes it seemed she had a new one every day, and the house began to fill up with them. Each emerged as more atrocious than the last; it was impossible to take any of them seriously. When asked by her friends at the nursing home how they had worked, my mother politely but truthfully told them that none of the wigs fitted me properly. With her heart in entirely the right place, one of my mother's closest co-workers offered the services of her wig maker, who would measure my head and make one 'just the way I wanted it, just like my real hair'. Not wanting to appear ungrateful, as coached by my mother, I thanked this woman and agreed to go, with the unspoken understanding between my mother and me that this was not something I actually wanted.

We drove to New City, a nearby town with a large Jewish population, and found the store amongst a small cluster of shops. I'd never been to a 'parlour' before, and somehow I'd envisioned a fancy salon filled with glamorous women, but instead the room was harshly lit with long overhead fluorescent bulbs, and instead of Warren Beatty, as I'd seen in *Shampoo*, the proprietor was a small old man who was bald himself. He affectionately beckoned me to sit in a chair facing a mirror framed with roughly carved pink and gold flowers. A large dusty rubber plant with leaves as big as my head filled one corner of the room.

'So, the little girl wants a wig, eh?'

He smiled at me in the mirror. I shrivelled inside, mortified beyond any realm I'd previously thought possible. He turned to my mother and they began speaking, his hand resting on my bird-thin shoulder. I kept watching him in the mirror, not because I was fascinated by him, but because I didn't want to look at myself. I knew the moment was coming when he'd ask me to take off my hat. I knew there was absolutely nothing I could do about it except pretend I didn't care, and when he turned back to me and the moment finally came, I took it off as nonchalantly as possible and placed it in my lap. I kept my gaze in the mirror directed on him while he took out a measuring tape and ran lines over the various angles of my head. I liked this part. My hair was growing out at that point, it was about half an inch long, and his dry hand stroked the baby-like fineness of it with a tenderness that made the back of my neck go all goose-flesh.

After the measuring, he went to the back room to get different samples. Knowing I'd had long blonde hair, he brought back wigs of varying lengths and shades of blonde ranging from bright yellow to almost brown. In turn he placed each one on and discussed with my mother which types were closest to my 'natural' state. He explained that all of the wigs were made of human hair, which made me envision a bizarre blend of the Christmas story, *The Journey of the Magi*, in which a woman sells for hair for the sake of love, and the Holocaust, where I knew they'd shaved the heads and kept the hair of people about to die horrible deaths.

Now it was unavoidable; I had to look at myself in the mirror. As each type of wig was put on and adjusted, both the man and my mother would ask me what I thought, but all I could manage was a sullen nod or shake of my head. Looking at myself in these wigs with their dull, however human hair, horrified me, and each time the man commented on 'how natural' it looked I only saw him, and eventually myself, as that much more alien.

How much longer was this going to go on? How many wigs in the world were there, anyway? Though inside I was growing more and more petulant, I made half-hearted efforts to look happy, and when the last wig was finally tried on, I actually smiled when the old man asked how I liked it. I hated it. At last, the issue of cost came up, which in my mind signalled the end of this charade. I knew my mother would never want to pay for something so ludicrous as a wig, and besides, hadn't we more or less agreed we were never really going to get one? The man quoted an astounding sum, something far higher than we could have even joked about. I sat there in the chair and watched the reflections of my mother and this man talking in the mirror, my feet swinging, ready to leave. To my great amazement, I saw a look on my mother's face that seemed to say she was actually considering ordering one of these over-priced, custom-made patches of hair. Could she really be serious? I looked on in astonishment, and when we finally left the store it was with a promise that she would think it over and call him tomorrow. Once in the car I thought she would look at me and we'd both laugh, share our private joke, but instead she turned and addressed me seriously, 'Well, do you want one? It's a lot of money, but if you want one, I'll buy it for you.'

What had happened? I thought we'd only gone to be polite to her friend. Wasn't it obvious how hideous those wigs were, how alarming? I didn't know how to reply. Back at home she called up her friend to tell her what had happened and I heard her say, 'It was the first time in a long while I've seen her smile. She hasn't smiled in so long.'

So that was it. Normally I was intuitive and could guess what was going on behind people's words and actions, but if my own mother could be so wrong about my actions, how could I know I too wasn't mistaken in my own interpretations?

Before this got too far out of hand, I took it upon myself to go to my mother and tell her outright that I didn't want a wig, that I thought they were ugly. She looked relieved, because of the expense, but as she looked at me and smiled I thought again of what she'd said over the phone. I smiled again at her, sick within my own heart at this newly discovered chasm opening up between me and the rest of the world, as if there weren't enough chasms already. But out of my compulsion continually to seek out the truth I questioned her about her conversation with her friend, which amounted to her betrayal of me. I insisted I was okay, happy even, that the wig was a big joke. She smiled back at me even more broadly, relieved to see my old self, and for that moment I actually was happy, content that I could give her at least that.

I kept on wearing my hat. But I couldn't shake off the image of my own face staring back at me with that ludicrous, grotesque halo of a wig. Did they actually mean it when they said, 'Now doesn't that look nice?' I felt quite certain that I looked awful in those wigs, yet why did my belief not seem to match up with everyone else's? Were they lying to me? Perhaps they didn't want to hurt my feelings. It was dawning on me that I might look much worse than I had actually supposed.

One morning I went into the bathroom and shut the door behind me, despite the fact I was alone in the house. I turned on the lights and very carefully, very seriously, assessed my own face in the mirror. I was bald, but I knew that already. I also knew I had buck teeth, something I was vaguely ashamed of but hadn't given too much thought to until this moment. They were ugly. And, I noticed, they were made worse by the fact my chin seemed so small. How had it got that way? I didn't remember it being so small before. I rooted around in the cabinets and came up with a hand mirror and, with a bit of angling, looked, for the first time, at my right profile. I knew to expect a scar, but how had my face sunk in like that? I didn't understand. Was it possible I'd looked this way for a while and was only just noticing it, or was this something very recent? More than the ugliness I felt, I was suddenly appalled by the notion that I'd been walking around not aware of something apparent to everyone else. A profound sense of shame consumed me.

I put the mirror away, shut off the lights and went back into the living room and lay in the sunlight with the cats. They didn't care how I looked. I made a silent vow to love them valiantly, truly, with an intensity that would prove I was capable, worthy of . . . I wasn't sure of what, but of something wonderful, something noble, something spectacular. I repeated the same vow to the dogs.

My father worked odd hours, leaving late in the morning and not arriving home until long after dark. He'd cook his own dinner and eat it standing up near the sink while staring contemplatively out of the viewless and dark kitchen window. Some nights I'd get out of bed and go visit him there. He'd hear me pad into the room and stare at me, his face surprised for only a moment before it transformed into genuine pleasure at seeing me. 'Lucinda Mag,' he'd announce, as if he were only just then naming me, and I'd sit down on a chair, pulling my nightgown over my knees, stretching the material tight. He'd sit down at the table with me and eat in silence while I watched, both of us perfectly content. One night I walked in and he was wearing a wig. They littered the house by then and we'd grown careless with them. The cats slept on them, the dogs played tug of war, they were still good for a few laughs when visitors put them on. My father was standing over the stove, stirring a pan full of something sizzling. 'Lucinda Mag,' he announced, grinning, inviting me to tell him how silly he looked, which I didn't. I simply sat down as always and watched him finish cooking and eating his solitary meal until finally I couldn't stand it any more.

'Daddy, take it off.'

'Take what off?'

'The wig'.

'What wig, I'm not wearing a wig.'

'*Daddy*.'

'I have no idea what you're talking about.'

It went on like this. I knew he was joking, and I knew he had no idea how much I *really* wanted him to take the wig off. I gave up. Freeing my knees from my nightgown, I walked over to him, pushed the long hair aside and kissed him goodnight.

I was still experimenting, unsuccessfully, with making myself ill during the long mornings, mornings I never thought of as lonely. Pneumonia remained my pet plan, though I was still unable to inhale the water. Summer had arrived so there was no hope of catching cold outside, but I'd seen enough trapped-in-the-desert movies to hope for heatstroke. I didn't have a clue what heatstroke was, but the word stroke made me envision some sort kind of tender caress. I did know that it involved seeing mirages. Because of the extra radiation I wasn't allowed to go into the sun, so any exposure which might give me a tan was out.

I wrapped myself in a blanket and went to lie in my private spot in the back yard. I lay there and felt the ants crawl up on my skin. While I liked ants and bugs in general, I occasionally tortured them. I always felt guilty and sinful afterwards. Still, no number of vows ever seemed to stop me. I was finally cured after reading a German fairy tale that described a horrible little girl who liked to pull the wings off flies. When she died and went to purgatory she was doomed to have all the flightless little lives she'd ruined crawl all over her and get in her mouth, her eyes. I stopped my own torture not out of morality, but a combination of self-preservation and disgust.

Sunlight came in pinhole streams through the blanket. Birds and chainsaws sang and wailed in the background. It was sweltering. I sat up and pulled the blanket cowl-like around my head and stared into the distance. Sweat rolled down the side of my ribcage, a ribcage so skinny I could feel each drop momentarily rest above the ridge of each bone. I stared into the distance. I was looking for my mirage. In the movies they saw either water holes or beautiful women, sometimes both. My eyes scanned the back yard: nothing. My tee shirt was now drenched with sweat. Even the backs of my hands were sweating, even my scalp, which itched against the blanket. I realized this wasn't going to work. Lifting myself up with great effort, I walked back into the air-conditioned house, the wave of cold hitting my face like a bucket of water when I opened the door.

The one time I actually got out of having the chemotherapy, I wasn't even feeling particularly ill. But when the blood test came back with a high white blood cell count, I was overjoyed. It was decided I should be put into isolation for a bit, and a porter came down to the clinic to collect me in a wheelchair. I loved riding in wheelchairs, and waved gaily to Dr Woolf as I was chauffeured past him.

'Better not look too happy,' my mother advised me.

Immediately I went into my waif mode, a style I'd been perfecting for some time now. Since becoming slowly aware of my odd appearance, I'd decided to use it for all it was worth. It was the way I knew how to have an effect on people, to matter somehow.

Isolation wasn't such a thrill after all. Because my admission was unexpected, I hadn't come prepared with books or toys, and, horror or horrors, the room had no television. I wasn't permitted to have any of the ward's shabby toys brought into me because of germs, and there was no view because the only window was blocked by a broken air-conditioner. I kept opening the door to stick my head out, but some one always yelled at me to shut it, to stay inside and get back into bed. I felt perfectly fit. How could I really be ill? Lying face down on my bed, I felt my hip bones jut down into the over-starched sheets. Sleep was a long way off. I saved myself only by pretending I was a prisoner put 'in the hole', something I'd read about in a book about a group of men in prison, a book I knew I wasn't supposed to read because in it the men had sex with the prison's mascot, a donkey. I lay there and pretended I'd been framed.

That week was the exception, though. Most weeks the routine was the same, Friday was still D-day. The chemotherapy lasted for two and a half years. It became my entire life. It never occurred to me that it would one day end. In all those years there were probably only a handful of times when Dr Woolf was running on time. I'd go to the public bathroom down the hall just to fill the time. I loved the feeling of my small body travelling in the same direction as all those large bodies in suits and white jackets striding effortlessly past me, the street shoes clicking on the tile.

It was an old bathroom, and a small one with only two stalls. Each stall door was wooden and closed on the inside with a silvery metal latch. There was no graffiti anywhere in the bathroom except on these latches. Someone, certainly the same person, had scratched onto each rectangular piece of metal a message. Sitting on the toilet in the first stall you could read *God Is Near*, and on the second, *Be Here Now*. I always pictured whoever wrote these sitting there on the same porcelain as myself, bending forward, one arm raised up and resting against the warping wood of the door, a nail file in their other hand. I sensed they had done this a long time ago, before my time. What was wrong with them? I wondered, why were they here? I never asked myself what might have happened to them.

Still spending my private moments trying to engage God in conversations, alternately attempting to barter him into answering my questions and silently trying to listen to whatever the answer might be, these bathroom communications seemed important to me.

Each atrocious week I'd plod down to this bathroom, trying to kill time before the inevitable, and I'd pause for a moment before the two doors, trying to decide which message I wanted to read. *God Is Near*. Well, okay, how near? Did this mean he was near in the way someone is near when they're coming towards you, moving closer and closer, not yet here but to be expected sooner or later? Or did it mean he was near but not showing his face, present but unseeable, someone breathing quietly in a closet? *Be Here Now*. I didn't want to be here now. My wanting was inconsequential. I *was* here now, whether I liked it or not. But something about this saying attracted me, either despite or because of its seeming simplicity, and two out of three times I went for door number two.

Some weeks I stared at it dumbly, thinking only of what was happening back in the waiting room with my mother, how many more rows of knitting she'd finished. Some weeks I thought of the impending injection, or I simply continued on with my fantasy life: the Pony Express rider seeks relief in the town's Saloon, the Alien

84

ponders the wonders of waste disposal. Some weeks, especially when it was hot, I thought of nothing and only listened to my urine hiss into the water below my legs as I leaned forward, pressing the coolness of the inscribed metal against my forehead, and wept.

7

Masks

HAVING MISSED MOST of fourth grade and all but a week or so of fifth grade, I finally started re-emerging at school sometime in sixth grade, during my sporadic 'vacations' from chemo-therapy. Mysteriously showing up for a week or two weeks or sometimes even three or four, I'd disappear again for a couple of months. I wore my little white sailor's hat constantly, even when I was away from the chemo long enough actually to grow a fine inch of soft, baby-like hair.

Most of the sixth-grade class was composed of children I'd grown up with who were, for the most part, genuinely curious about what had happened to me. They treated me respectfully if not somewhat distantly, though there was always a clique of boys who called me names: 'Hey, girl, take off that monster mask: oops, she's not wearing a mask!' This was the height of hilarity in sixth grade and the boys, for they were always and only boys, practically fell to the ground, besotted with their own wit. Much to their bewilderment and to the shock of my teachers, I responded by calling out to them, 'You stupid dildos.'

Derek used to say that word all the time and I thought it a wonderful insult, though I didn't have a clue as to what a dildo was. After being reprimanded enough times for wielding this powerful insult, I finally asked my brother what it meant: an artificial penis, he informed me. I gave up using the word. I'd known children in the hospital with artificial limbs, and I'd also known children with urinary tract problems.

The school year progressed slowly. It seemed as if I had been in the sixth grade for years, yet it was only October. Halloween was coming up. Coming from Ireland, we had never treated it as a big holiday, though Sarah and I usually took part anyway. For the last couple of years I hadn't even been able to go out, having always been too sick. But this year it fell on a day when I felt quite fine. My mother was the one who came up with the Eskimo idea. I put on a winter coat, made a fish out of paper which I hung on the end of a stick, and wrapped my face up in a scarf. My hair was growing out, and I loved the way the top of the hood rubbed against it.

We walked around the neighbourhood with our pillowcase sacks, running into other groups of kids and comparing notes: the house three doors down gave whole candy bars while the house next door to that only gave cheap mints. I felt wonderful, but it was only gradually, as the night wore on and the moon came out and the older kids, the big kids, went on their round that I began to realize why I felt so good. No one could see me clearly. No one could see my face.

It was a very warm end of October and I was sweating in my parka, but I didn't care. I felt such freedom: I waltzed up to people effortlessly and boldly, I asked questions and made comments the rest of my troupe were too afraid to make. I didn't understand their fear. I hadn't realized just how meek I'd become, how self-conscious I was about my appearance until now when it was obscured. My sister and her friends' appearances, or so it seemed from my perspective, were never a problem, so why didn't they always feel as bold and as happy as I felt that night?

Our sacks filled up and eventually it was time to go home. We gleefully poured out our candy on the floor and traded off: because chewing had become difficult, I gave Sarah everything too hard for me, while she unselfishly gave me everything soft. I took off my Eskimo parka and went down to my room, not wearing my hat. Normally, I didn't feel that I had to wear my hat around my family, and I never wore it when I was alone in my room. Yet, once I was alone with all that candy, still hot from running around on that unseasonably warm night, I felt compelled to put my hat back on. I didn't know what was wrong. I ate sugar until I was ready to burst, trying hard to ignore everything except what was directly in front of me, what I could touch and taste, the chocolate melting brown beneath my fingernails, the candy so sweet it made my throat hurt.

The following spring, on one of the first warm days, I was playing with an old friend, Teresa, in her neat and ordered back yard when completely out of the blue she asked if I was dying. She looked at me casually, as if she'd just asked me what I was doing later that day. 'The other kids say that you're slowly dying, that you're "wasting away".' I looked at her in shock. Dying? Why on earth would anyone think I was dying? 'No,' I replied, in the same tone of voice as if she'd asked me whether or not I was the Pope, 'I'm not dying.'

I planned on asking my mother why Teresa would say such a thing when I got home. But just as I was coming through the front door, she was entering from the garage door, her arms laden with shopping bags. I was still a tomboy at heart and cared little about what I wore, just so long as it wasn't a dress.

My mother took a bright red shirt out of the bag and held it up against my chest. It smelled new and a price tag scratched my neck. 'Turtlenecks are very hard to find in short sleeves, so I bought you several.' Turtlenecks, why on earth would I want to wear turtlenecks in the spring? I didn't ask this out loud, but my mother must have known what I was thinking. She looked me straight in the eye: 'If you wear something that comes up around your neck, it makes the scar less visible.'

Genuinely bewildered, I took the brightly coloured pile of clothes down to my room. Wouldn't I look even more stupid wearing a turtleneck in the summer? Would they really hide my 'scar'? I knew that I looked different from other people, but I remained unclear as to the exact details of this difference. I hadn't taken a good, long, objective look at myself since the wig fitting, but that seemed so long ago, almost two years. I remembered feeling upset by it, but conveniently didn't remember what exactly it was I'd seen in that mirror, and I hadn't allowed myself a close scrutiny since. Not particularly concerned with my looks, which was partly a result of my sixth-grade tomboy nature, I managed to live outside the mirror's reflection.

I donned my short-sleeved turtlenecks and finished out the few short months left of elementary school. I played with my friend Jan at her wonderful home with its few acres of meadow and, most magnificent of all, a small lake. There was a rowboat we weren't really allowed to take out by ourselves, but we did anyway. Rowing it to the far shore, a mere eighth of a mile away, we'd 'land' and pretend we'd just discovered a new country. With notebooks in hand, we logged our discoveries, overturning stones and giving false Latin names to the newts and various pieces of slime we found under them.

Jan had as complex a relationship to her stuffed and plastic animals as I had to mine, and when I slept over we'd compare our intricate worlds. Sometimes Jan wanted, though not too frequently, to talk about boys, and I sat there on my sleeping bag with my knees tucked up under my nightgown, listening patiently. I never had too much information to offer, though I had just developed my very first crush. It was on Omar Sharif.

Late one night I'd stayed up and watched *Dr Zhivago* on television with my father. Curling up beside him and laying my head against his big stomach, I listened to my father's heart, his breathing, and attentively watched the images of a remote world, a world that was as beautiful as it was deadly and cold. I thought I would have managed very well there, imagined that I would have remained true to my passions had I lived through the Russian Revolution. I, too, would have trudged across all that tundra, letting the ice sheet over me and crackle on my eyebrows. For weeks I pictured the ruined estate where Zhivago wrote his sonnets, aware that the true splendour of the house lay inextricably bound to the fact it was ruined. I didn't understand why this should be so, and I didn't understand why re-imagining this scene gave me such a deep sense of fulfilment, nor why this fulfilment was mingled with such a sad sense of longing, nor why this longing only added to the beauty of everything else.

Elementary School Graduation Day approached. I remembered being in second grade and looking out on a group of sixth graders preparing for graduation. It had seemed like such an unimaginable length of time to me before I'd get there, so long, so unreal. But now I was out there mingling in the courtyard, remembering the day when I actually laid my head down on the desk and announced to the teacher, 'I'll never make it.' I could even see the classroom window which I had gazed out of. So much had happened in four years. I felt so old, and I felt proud of being so old. During the ceremony I was shocked when the vice-principal started speaking about *me*, about how I should receive special attention for 'my bravery'. I could feel the heat rising in me as he spoke, my face turning red. Here I was, the centre of attention, receiving the praise and appreciation I'd been fantasizing about for so many years, and all I could feel was intense, searing embarrassment. I was called up onto the platform. I know everyone was applauding, but I felt it more than heard it. In a daze I reached out and accepted the gift Mr Schultz was presenting me with, a copy of *The Prophet*. I could barely thank him.

Later, alone in my room, I opened the book at random. The verse I read was about love, about how to accept the love of another with dignity. I shut the book after only a page. I wanted nothing to do with the world of love; I thought wanting love was a weakness to be overcome. and, besides, I thought to myself, the world of love wanted nothing to do with me.

The summer passed and entrance into Junior High School was looming. Jan, Teresa and Sarah were all very excited at the prospect of being 'grown-ups', of attending different classes, of having your own locker. Their excitement was contagious and on the night before the first day of school, I proudly marked my assorted notebooks for my different subjects and secretly scuffed my new shoes to make them look old.

Everyone must have been nervous, but I was sure I was the only one who felt apprehension. I found myself sidling through the halls I'd been looking forward to, trying to pretend that I didn't notice the other kids, almost all of them strangers from adjoining towns, staring at me. I had been looking forward to going to the lunch room, having seen enough teen movies with their promise of intrigue and drama, only to sit down next to a table full of boys.

They pointed openly and laughed, calling out loud enough for me to hear. '*What* on earth is *That*?' '*That* is the ugliest girl I have *ever* seen.' I knew in my heart that their comments had nothing to do with me, that it was all about them appearing tough and cool to their friends. But these boys were older than the ones in grade school and, for the very first time, I realized they were passing judgement on my suitability, or lack of it, as a girlfriend.

'I bet David wants to kiss her, don't you David?' 'Yeah, right, then I'll kiss your mother's asshole.' 'How'll you know which is which?'

My initial tactic was to pretend I didn't hear them, but this only seemed to spur them on. In the hallways, where I suffered similar teasing from random attackers, I simply looked down at the floor and walked more quickly, but in the lunch room I was a sitting duck. The same group took to seeking me out and purposefully sitting near me day after day, even when I tried to camouflage myself by sitting in the middle of a group. They grew bolder and I could hear them plotting to send someone to come and sit across from me. I'd look up from my food and there would be a boy slouching awkwardly in a red plastic chair, innocently asking me my name. Then he'd ask me how I got to be so ugly. At this the group would burst into laughter, and my inquisitor would saunter back, victorious.

It only took two weeks before I finally broke down and went to my guidance counsellor to complain. I thought he would offer to reprimand them, but instead he asked if I'd like to come and eat in the privacy of his office. Surprised, I said yes, and that's what I did whenever I was attending school for the rest of the year. Every day I'd wait for him, the other guidance counsellors and the secretaries to go out on their own lunch breaks. Then I'd walk through the empty outer office and sit down in his private office, closing the door behind me. As I ate the food inside my brown paper bag, which crinkled loudly in the silence, I'd look at the drawings his own young children had made. They were taped to the wall near his desk, simplistic drawings in which the sky was a blue line near the top and the grass a green line near the bottom and people were as big as houses. I felt safe and secure in that office, but I also felt lonely, and for the very first time I definitely identified the source of my unhappiness as being the fact that I was ugly. A few weeks later I left school to re-enter chemotherapy and, also for the very first time, was even vaguely glad to go back to it.

My inner life became ever more macabre. Vietnam was still within recent memory and pictures of the horrors of Cambodia loomed on every TV screen and in every newspaper. I told myself again and again how good I had it in comparison, what a wonder it was to have food and clothes and a home and no one torturing me. I told myself what fools those boys at school were, what stupid, unaware lives they led. How could they assume their own lives were so important? Didn't they know that they could lose everything at any moment, that you couldn't take anything good or worthwhile for granted, because pain and cruelty could and would arrive sooner or later? I bombed and starved and persecuted my own suffering right out of existence.

I had the capacity of imagination to escape my own pain momentarily, and I had the elegance of imagination to teach myself something true regarding the world around me, but I didn't yet have the clarity of imagination to grant myself the complicated and necessary right to suffer. I treated despair in terms of hierarchy: if there was a more important pain in the world, it meant my own was to be negated. I thought I simply had to accept the fact that I was ugly, and that to feel despair about such a thing was simply wrong.

Halloween came round again and even though I was feeling a bit woozy from an injection I'd had just a few days before, I begged my mother to let me go out. I put on a plastic witch mask and went out with Teresa. I walked down the streets suddenly bold and free: no one could see my face. I peered through the oval eye slits and did not see one person staring back at me, ready to make fun of my face. I breathed in the condensing, plastic tainted air behind the mask and thought that I was breathing in normalcy, that this freedom and ease were what the world was composed of, that other people felt it all the time. How could they not? How could they not understand and feel the joy of walking down the street without a single threat of being made fun of? Assuming this was how other people felt all the time, I again marked my own face as the thing which kept me apart, as the tangible element of what was wrong with my life, and with me. At home, when I finally took the mask off, I felt both sad and relieved. Sad because I had felt like a pauper walking for a few brief hours in the clothes of a prince and because I had liked it so much. Relieved because I felt no connection with that kind of happiness: I didn't deserve it and thus I shouldn't want it. It was easier to slip back into my depression and blame my face for everything.

Hanna was a cleaning woman in Dr Woolf's office. She was quite old, or at least seemed old to me, and she always wore a cardigan, summer and winter. Her domain, when she wasn't polishing the hallway floors or disinfecting various pieces of metal furniture, was an oblong room off the main doctors' hallway, just a few doors down from Dr Woolf's. I appreciated this room because it was painted pale blue, so unlike the sickly green which dominated the rest of the place. The last year or so of chemotherapy I'd grown considerably weaker and sometimes walking the few blocks to the parking lot, after the injection was over, seemed insurmountable. On particularly bad days my mother would leave me in Hanna's care while she went to fetch the car. Hanna would sit me down in a chair next to a small table with a kettle and some cups on it, a small island of her own where she took breaks.

The routine never varied. She knelt in front of me and asked, 'How do you feel?' I could hear her slip rubbing between her stockings and dress. Looking her straight in the eyes I'd dutifully report, 'My nose hurts.'

It was always such a relief to be able to admit this to her. I would later discover why the chemo had affected my sinuses, but as far as I could tell, Hanna appeared to be the only one at the time who believed this comic complaint. She'd nod sympathetically and offer me a cup of tea, the last thing in the world I wanted. I politely refused. Then we would just simply sit there and stare at each other, waiting for my mother to return. I knew that beyond a cup of tea, there was nothing she could offer me. But her gaze soothed me. Normally I despised the looks of others, but with Hanna I felt a vague sense of camaraderie, imagining that both our little lives were made miserable by these unknowing, cloddish doctors. To her I was probably just one more of the sick children who streamed in and out of the place, though in my mind I'd found a silent link with someone, someone whose life was as difficult as I found my own. As ill as I felt, I always liked sitting there with her, imagining our parallel lives clicking quietly along like two trains beside each other, two trains with similar routes but different destinations.

When I played with Jan or Teresa, my friends from that time now irretrievably known as *Before*, they treated me the same way they always had, though perhaps with an air of delicacy which seemed uncomfortable and unnatural for all of us. They asked me questions about the physical side of things, how much it hurt, why was I so skinny, when my hair would grow back, and I loved to answer them with vigour and embellishment. One third of my answers were shaped by the braggart's love of a good tale, another third because I instinctively knew they'd never understand what it was really like, and the last third because I myself didn't really know what it was like a great deal of the time. I witnessed my life unfolding like someone who's awkwardly stumbled in after the movie has already started. I sensed something important had been revealed in the opening sequence, some essential knowledge everyone else was privy to that was being kept from me.

I could converse with well-intended neighbours, go the usual round of polite questions about my health, though I was highly aware of how different these conversation were from the ones with my friends on Ward Ten, my friends from *After*. People who weren't ill, or not involved in the daily flow of hospital life, had their own ideas of what it was like to be ill. It seemed impossible ever to tell them how it really was, and doing so did not seem particularly desirable to me. I preferred it if strangers on the street imagined me sickly, confident that as soon as I was back on Ward Ten my friends and I would utterly redefine for each other the concept of what it was like to be sick.

I felt as if my illness was a blanket the world had thrown over me; all that could be seen from the outside was an indistinguishable lump. And somehow I transformed that blanket into a tent, beneath which I almost happily set up camp. I had no sense of how my life was *supposed* to be, only of how it was. Not that this meant that I was actually happy, not in any normal definition of the word. Though I depended on my apocalyptic thoughts to keep my own situation in perspective, they did imbue me with a rather depressed aura. 'For God's sake, stop looking so morbid all the time,' became a familiar phrase in my house. Whenever anyone else was present I found myself incapable of being anything other than a depressed lump. It was only when I was alone, in utter privacy, that my ability to relish life surfaced.

For the longest time every day of the week was just one long dreadful slide towards Friday, counting off the number of days that separated me from the next injection. In the horribly familiar cycle, all of Friday night and most of Saturday morning was spent throwing up, I was an expert now on throwing up. Saturday night the nausea would begin to abate, though only, it seemed, so I could concentrate that much more on how badly my head throbbed. Sunday I hardly threw up at all, and though my head still pounded, I discovered brief moments of relief, a reprieve, always towards evening, signalling that all the pain would end in twenty-four hours, more or less.

I never knew when that moment would come exactly, it surprised me each time. Normally if I wanted to go to the bathroom it required thinking ahead, slowly, ever so slowly, pulling the covers off and rotating into position to sit up. Delicately, I'd pull my torso into a vertical position while at the same time gingerly pivoting my legs towards the floor. I knew to expect a horrific wave of dizziness and stomach ache when I stood up, and so intent was I in preparing for it that the time when it *didn't* come, left me flabbergasted. I'd stand up from my bed utterly prepared to feel terrible, and instead I'd catch a glimpse of how it was to *not* feel terrible. I knew also from hard-bought experience that even though I'd usually feel awful by the time I actually did make it to the bathroom, the possibility of being well in my body existed and would eventually return.

Each week, with each first glimmer of returning strength, I discovered that, for me, joy could be measured in negative terms: of what I *didn't* have, which was pain and weakness. I discovered the greatest happiness wasn't something I acquired through some sort of effort, it was something I already had, deep and sonorous inside me, and that it was found through a process of removing the walls of pain around it. I knew the walls were inside me, and I saw that most people, never having experienced any sort of deep physical discomfort on a regular basis, didn't, couldn't know this.

I viewed other people both critically and sympathetically. Why couldn't they just stop complaining so much, just let go and see how good they actually had it? It seemed to me that everyone was always waiting for something to happen which would then allow them to move forward, to get to the place they thought they wanted to be. They seemed to be waiting for some shadowy future moment to begin their lives in earnest. Everybody from my mother to the characters I read about in books (who were as actual and as important as real people to me) was always looking at someone else's life and envying it, wishing they could occupy it. I wanted them to stop, to see how much they had already, how they had their health and their strength. I imagined how my life would be if I had half of their fortune. Then I would catch myself, guilty of exactly the thing I was accusing others of. As clear-headed as I could be, sometimes it seemed to me that the only reason for this clarity was to see how hypocritically I lived my own life.

Once, during a week of intensive chemotherapy, towards the end of the two and a half years, I was sent to a strange ward as Ten was already full when I checked in. My roommate was a girl who'd been run over by an ice boat; the blades had cut her intestines in two and she'd had to have them sewn back together. She got a lot of attention, lots of calls from concerned relatives and school friends, and I was both a little jealous of her and a little contemptuous because she was taking her accident a bit too seriously for my taste. After all, she lived, didn't she? She'd had one operation and maybe they were going to do another one next week, but after that it would all be over, so what was the big fuss about?

It was late at night, always a bad time in the hospital but especially on this ward, which I'd been on before, and which was notoriously understaffed. All of the wards were understaffed at night. Often there was only one nurse and a handful of aides to take care of everyone. This was particularly bad news if you had an IV. They were still using regular old butterfly needles, instead of the flexible catheter-type needles they have today. These were inserted into the back of your hand and simply taped down to the skin. The chances of it puncturing the vein were high, and I'd learned to keep whichever hand it was in absolutely still, even in my sleep. Worse, however, was the fact that the limited staff neglected to refill the IV bottles regularly, causing them to dry up in the night, clotting the needle with blood. There were many nights when I would have to be woken three or four times in order to be re-stuck with a new butterfly. My veins were so tired that often it took three, four, even five sticks before the doctor, who was never happy to be woken to do something as menial as set up an IV, could get the fluid to flow properly. I learned not only to sleep without moving, for fear of hitting the needle out of place, but also in two-hour shifts, so that I could wake up regularly and check the bottle's fluid level myself.

This particular night I woke up on that strange ward – and looked at the bottle in the blocks of light coming in through the city window. To my relief the glass bottle was still half full. The light coming in passed through the clear solution and threw a marbled reflection down on the floor. I had to go to the bathroom. I tried to assess if I could walk there unaided – it was only a few feet away – and decided I couldn't. Pressing the call button for a nurse, I sighed, realizing it wasn't a buzzer system as they had on other floors, but simply a bulb which would light up over my door outside in the hallway. Chances were good no one would see it for some time. I waited. I waited and waited and even tried calling out, but there was no chance of my voice carrying that far. My roommate slept soundly, still heavily sedated from her operation that morning. I saw her open mouth, her fat cheeks, her whole face turned upward towards the ceiling as her thick and curly hair fell to the side.

She'd spent all of yesterday's dinner time telling me about her parents' divorce, about how her father came to get her each weekend and always took her to do something. This weekend they'd been ice sailing. She spoke of it in a passive yet unhappy voice. While she was in surgery I listened to her mother fight with her father, accusing him of causing the accident. He yelled back at her and, in my mind, won. They all seemed very impressed with the complications of their lives, with their divorce and their fights and their daughter who commanded the divided attention of her parents. Who would ever understand how jealous I was?

I kept waiting to see if a nurse would come. How much time passed I don't know, but it was getting serious and I had to make a decision: get up and walk or pee in the bed. I'd done this once before in a similar situation. There was a brief time during my father's unemployment when I'd gone on Medicaid and was sent to a completely different part of the hospital, to a gigantic open ward disturbingly understaffed. I called and called for a nurse or an aide, but finally I couldn't stand it any longer and, with great relief, let go and peed right there in the bed. I had to lie in it until it was cold and had spread through all of the sheets before someone finally, almost comically, walked in with a bedpan. The person holding the bedpan looked at me disapprovingly and said she'd send someone to change my sheets. Ten minutes later a woman showed up and looked at me in surprise. She asked me how old I was and when I told her eleven she shook her head and said when she'd heard someone'd peed in their bed, she thought it must have been a baby.

I wasn't going to go through that embarrassment again. All I had to do was be strong, I told myself, and I could make it to the bathroom. Sitting up wasn't hard at all. Slipping down to the floor was fine as long as I did it slowly. Grabbing hold of my IV pole, which was troublesomely on the wrong side of the bed, adding extra length to the journey, I began the seven or eight steps to the bathroom. I passed the foot of my own bed. Traffic was still audible outside, even at this hour. My sleeping roommate breathed heavily, almost snoring but not quite, while my IV swayed and clinked against the metal pole as I pushed it along. I neared the foot of her bed and had almost passed it when I understood I would never make it. I was exhausted. I had to sit down but the one chair in the room was even further away than the bathroom or my bed. Tiredness and a creeping ache so overwhelmed me that I forgot I even had to go to the bathroom. Could I make it back to my bed? It was too far. Suddenly afraid I was going to faint, I crouched down to the floor, aware that I'd adopted the same pose as the crouched skeletal figures in the countless famine pictures I studied so hard in news magazines. *I'm okay* I told myself, *I'm okay*.

I thought that if I could just rest like that for long enough, I'd regain adequate strength to make it back to the bed, only about five feet away. It might as well have been five miles. My knees began to ache and afraid I might fall even from this crouch position, and in the process dislodge the IV, I gingerly lay down on the floor. My hip bones and elbows hurt against the hard floor. If I lay here long enough, would someone come by and see me? After all, my call light was still on. What would they think, seeing me lying here? Maybe they'd feel sorry for me, maybe they'd sweep me up in their arms, place me back in bed and lay a comforting hand across my forehead, whisper something sweet and consoling in my ear.

Until that moment I believed in the drama of my life or the

dramatic possibilities my tragedy called up. Except, now, the floor was cold. The floor was just so cold. I really didn't want to lie there any more, and even though it would take an Herculean effort to ease myself back up – an effort that would dispel my comforting notions about my own helplessness and lack of responsibility – the floor was cold and I didn't want to wait any more for someone to come and rescue me. For the very first time, I had a glimmer of what that person had meant when they scratched their message into the bathroom door, eleven floors below: *Be Here Now*. I felt a bottomless sense of peace, of stillness. I decided it was simply a matter of will, that if I really concentrated, I could make it back. And I did. It took a long time and I don't remember anything once I was back in bed. I must have fallen asleep immediately, only to be woken from a deep sleep a little while later by an aide, answering my call light at last.

'Do you realize this is the last six weeks?' my mother asked late one Thursday afternoon while starting to prepare dinner.

'What?'

'The last set of shots. Only six more and then all this will be over. What a relief. You must be overjoyed.'

I was shocked. Over? It was almost over? I looked at her, speechless. 'Thank God for that,' I said, using a phrase she employed all the time.

I went down to my room and lay on my bed, utterly confused. Why wasn't I overjoyed? I was almost thirteen years old. I'd been doing this since I was ten; I barely remembered what life had been like before. No more shots, no more Dr Woolf, no more throwing up. I was afraid, and I was afraid that I was afraid. Why wasn't I happy, the way I was supposed to be? What was wrong with me? I didn't want it to continue, did I? No, I knew I didn't, but life without it, after it, seemed unimaginable to me. Bewilderment filled the room and, as hard as it was for me to admit this to myself, I knew I was afraid of it ending, of everything changing. I wouldn't be special any more, no one would love me. Without the arena of chemotherapy in which to prove myself, how would anyone know I was worthy of love? But how could I ever want the chemotherapy to go on? I lay there turning these things over and over in my mind, more perplexed than I'd ever been in my entire life.

Counting off the days became an obsession for me. Thirty-eight more days until the last shot. Thirty-two more days. Fifteen more days. Three days and eighteen hours. Forty-eight hours and nineteen minutes. Three hours. Sixteen minutes. Now. I walked into Dr Woolf's office and it didn't seem in any way special, in any way different. It was a bit grey outside, a bit chilly, but not exactly cold. Dr Woolf was all business as usual, on the phone, talking in five different directions at once. For only the second time in two and a half years, I looked at the syringes in the basin. There were two of them, and one of them was filled with a bright red solution, the colour of Kool Aid. I watched him attach the needles, watched him walk carelessly around the room with them, still on the phone but to someone different now. Then he put the phone down and put the tourniquet on and rubbed my arm with a cotton ball, the smell of rubbing alcohol filling the air. As usual, it took a few stabs to find a vein, but the third one worked.

The hot flashes came, followed by the familiar nausea, and I painfully retched up nothing but the single Thorazine pill I'd been given an hour before. It was meant to help the vomiting, but every week I only threw it up, and there it was again, half dissolved, pinging into the basin. Slowly, it dawned on me that I wasn't crying. These last few months I hardly cried at all: it wasn't that I actually cried less, but that I controlled it more. Not crying had become the *raison d'être* of my visits to the chemotherapy clinic. But now, I felt absolutely nothing. My mother was praising me for being so good. I looked at her and at the beautiful window behind her. Robotically, I looked back to my arm, to Dr Woolf's huge hands changing syringes. Nothing. I felt only a void. Even the usual pain floated around me. It seemed to belong more to the room than to me, and even then awkwardly, like a clumsy piece of furniture.

Then it was over. My mother and Dr Woolf were speaking with each other. I couldn't hear them though they were right there next to me. Instead, I was looking at the ceiling. It was peeling and there was a water stain just a little bit off to the right. Funny, I thought to myself, all that time looking around and never having noticed the ceiling. Had I never looked at it, or had I looked at it dozens of times, only now really *seeing* it? My mother finished speaking with Dr Woolf, turned towards me and then she, too, before helping me off the table, wordlessly looked up for a moment, following the direction of my gaze.

She went off to get the car and I was ushered into Hanna's room. 'How do you feel?' she asked. I began to cry. Just a little bit at first, but soon I was sobbing and my whole body was shaking. I tried to stop, but it was out of control, and I gave myself over to it. Hanna bent over me and put an arm on my shoulder for a second, only for a second, then withdrew it and straightened up. She stood there for a few moments holding her hands together over her stomach, then without asking busied herself making me the cup of tea she'd been offering me for years. Through my sobs, which were getting loud now, I heard the water rattle and hiss inside the electric kettle. My lungs were already filled with sorrow and though I didn't think it was possible, I cried even harder.

A few minutes later, Hanna handed me the tea. It was in a mug with a picture of the Statue of Liberty on it. Holding the hot mug in my hands, I cried just as hard but conscious now that I mustn't spill the tea. My head was pounding. Slowly, I realized it was beginning to stop. I felt so tired all of a sudden, but quietly tired, in a restful way, not the usual exhaustion. By the time my mother returned, I had stopped crying, though not because of any effort on my part, just because it had run its natural course. We said goodbye to Hanna and walked out. No one on the streets, busy bending their heads down into the cold wind, seemed to notice or care that this day was different from others.

8

Truth and Beauty

M Y HAIR WAS growing out, but I still wore my little white
sailor's hat constantly. It was a security measure. I felt naked
without it. I tried not to think about it too much, but I figured my
ugliness could still be attributed to my hair. It wasn't long enough,
it was still too fine: there were many reasons to keep the hat on.
There were all kinds of wild rumours at school about what was
underneath it.

Finally, a full three or four inches of hair later, just as I was
leaving the house with Susie to go someplace I turned around to
run back up the stairs, calling out, 'Just a minute while I get my
hat.' 'You don't need it any more, Lucy, your hair is fine, come on
already,' she called back to me, frustrated that we were going to be
late. I stopped in the middle of the stairs and, genuinely surprised,
considered what she had said. Running my fingers through it, I had
to admit she was more or less right. It was nowhere near the length
it used to be, but there was no getting around it: I wasn't bald.
Turning around, I went out with her into the world, bareheaded
for the first time in years. There was a warm and gusty breeze
outside which parted my hair and stroked it like a caress. We went
to the store and people gave me second looks as they always did,
but not one person called me Baldy.

The next day I went to school bareheaded and not one person
mentioned it. Had I been wrong in thinking that I needed to hide
behind my hat, had it all been a mistake on my part? Except,
people still looked at me. Though I had given up eating in the lunch
room, there were plenty of other relentless, daily attacks of teasing
in the hallways. Girls never teased me, but I could see them staring
at me out of the corner of my eye, and when I turned towards

them, they glanced away as quickly as they could, trying to pretend there was something else they were busily concentrating on. I'd catch adults staring at me outside school all the time. I played games with them in stores, positioning myself just so and pretending I was absorbed in examining some piece of merchandise, only to turn my head quickly and trap them as they averted their embarrassed stare. Groups of boys were what I most feared, and I gladly ducked into whatever empty doorway was at hand if I saw any coming my way that looked like trouble. It was easy to spot potential offenders: there was a certain swagger, a certain sway in the way they walked.

However tinged the relief was at leaving the familiar and well-ordered world of the hospital, it didn't last very long. The radiation had been very hard on my teeth, the lower ones especially, and I was going to need a lot of work done if they were to be saved. Because it was specialized work, it meant yet again, only a few short months after I naively thought I'd said goodbye to Columbia Presbyterian Hospital forever, that we had to start the routine of driving in once or twice a week again for what turned out to be two years' worth of dental work. The Dental Clinic was in a completely different part of the hospital, though we still walked through the same courtyard which Dr Woolf's office looked out onto. The hospital laundry was somewhere nearby and the smell of it, which I associated with the walk to Dr Woolf's, never failed to make me just a little bit queasy.

There was, however, the benefit of getting out of school. By now I hated school with a vengeance and would continually tell lies about my health in order to stay away. Anything just not to have to face those boys each day. Luckily, my mother was fairly compliant and, looking back, it's a wonder I was even allowed to pass into the eighth grade at all with my attendance record.

From all the various procedures, which included at least a dozen root canals, I was in a good amount of pain most of the time. Codeine was prescribed. We kept the refillable prescription bottle in a kitchen cabinet, and within a short while I was taking pills almost constantly, even when I wasn't in pain. The pleasant, sleepy feeling it offered became one of the things I looked forward to. No matter how bad I felt about the world, about my position in it, I felt safe and secure and even vaguely happy only thirty or forty minutes after I'd downed a couple of pills. As the months wore on and that pleasant effect became harder and harder to achieve, and as each pill seemed to touch the pain itself less and less, I started taking more and more pills. I was aware that I was taking more than I should, up to four times the regular dose, and took to alternately asking my mother and then my father to refill the prescription in order to keep my high consumption less conspicuous. They both noticed the pills seemed to be disappearing quickly, but assumed my brothers were pilfering them on the sly. All of this came to an abrupt end one day when my mother caught me in the act of sneaking out no less than six times the prescribed amount of pills into my palm. From then on I had to make do with aspirin.

My inability to open my mouth very wide caused a lot of problems whenever anyone wanted to work on my back teeth, and it was decided I should be admitted to the hospital and have a whole slew of work done all at once while under general anaesthesia. This idea was fine by me. Not only did it offer even more days off from school, but the thought of surgery seemed far more appealing to me than sitting wide awake in that dreadful dentist's chair.

This was my fifth operation, a number which seemed enormous at the time. A student nurse gripped my hand tightly, almost too tightly, squeezing the blood from my fingers, as a regular nurse injected my thighs with the pre-med. I still hated this part of the routine. My thighs would ache and sting from the medication, though I knew the waiting before the nurse walked in with the needles was the worst part of all. On the morning of the operation, an aide woke me early and tossed a surgical gown and a small bottle of betadine on my bed. I was to wash my whole body and my hair with this iodine solution, put on the gown and then wait in bed until the nurses came with the pre-med needles. The waiting felt endless, crowded with an unspoken dialogue inside my head concerning the nature of pain.

It gave me pleasure to think of the boys who teased me openly at school and the adults who stared at me covertly elsewhere, to think that they would never be able to stand this pain, that they would crumple. My whole body was tense and my stomach upside down, but I was convinced that because I did not admit these things, did not display them for others to see, it meant I actually had a chance at *really* being brave, not just pretending. Every time I heard footfalls coming down the hall, fear's physical rush would swell inside me, and as the footfalls passed my room a physical sense of relief overcame me. These false alarms, however, only heightened my fear, since I knew that sooner or later the approaching steps would really be for me.

Paradoxically, the moment after the injection came as a relief; every tension fell and floated prettily away like leaves from an autumn tree. As the minutes passed the sweet and strange comfort of the medication lifted me up and floated me around the room, and when the orderly finally arrived and asked me to slide over onto the stretcher, it seemed as if I were watching someone else shyly try to hold the short gown down over her legs as she awkwardly wiggled herself along the rough sheets.

When the operation was over I remember throwing up some swallowed blood and feeling terribly weak, though joyously relieved it was all over. In post-op, the specially trained nurses checked on me every ten minutes. I was too groggy to sense exactly what was going on, but I realised the aura of attention, the cool hands on my warm arms, the way my name distantly sounded in their soft, I-won't-let-anything-bad-happen-to-you voices, the notion that I was somehow special, that I mattered. But afterwards, when I was transported back to my room, I found myself dozing and waking for hours, each time more panicked at being all alone than before. I'd make up some excuse to ring for a nurse, just to have someone enter the room. I began to wish that the operation wasn't over, that I was still asleep on the stretcher with a crowd of people hovering near me. It got so that, as the number of operations I underwent increased, even when I was home in my own bed, upset about something, about how much I hated my face, I could put myself to sleep by imagining myself lying on a stretcher. It was as if I could hear the movements of strangers in comfortingly familiar uniforms all around me, the distant beeps which were really heartbeats, and the mechanical shushes of respirators which meant someone, somewhere near, was breathing.

It wasn't without a certain amount of shame that I took this kind of emotional comfort from surgery: after all, it was a bad thing to have an operation, wasn't it? Was there something wrong with me that I should find such a comfort in being taken care of so? Did it mean I *liked* having operations and thus that I deserved them?

Thanks to all this dental work, I was missing a great deal of school, where the taunts were becoming only harder to take. Somehow I had reasoned that if a bad thing happened often enough it got easier. That was the way it worked with pain, so why wasn't it working with teasing? Every time I was teased, which happened every day, usually several times a day at school, it just seemed incrementally more painful. I was good at not listening, at pretending I hadn't heard, but I could sense myself changing, becoming more fearful. Before I'd always been an outgoing person, and in the right circumstances I still was, but meeting new people was now laced with dread. Except for the one time I went to my guidance counsellor to complain, I discussed this with no one. Besides, I reasoned, what could I do about it? I was ugly so people were going to make fun of me simply because I *was* so ugly, so I'd just better get used to it. But I couldn't. No matter how much I braced myself, the words stung every time they were thrown at me. Although I thought it should make it less painful, it didn't seem to matter that I was doing everything I could to know the truth, to own the fact I was ugly, to make sure I was prepared for it, expecting to be told nothing I didn't already know.

I went to the hospital one afternoon for some outpatient surgery. A tooth in the back of my mouth had to be pulled and I was to be knocked out for about ten minutes. Afterwards, I was waiting in Recovery for my mother to take me home. She came in and pulled the blood-soaked gauze out of my mouth and gasped. In the course of the surgery two of my lower front teeth had been partially knocked out, leaving behind two very ugly stumps. It appeared that no one had been planning to tell either one of us about this complication, and it was only chance that my mother discovered it while we were still there. Justifiably, she exploded in anger. Predictably, the surgeon's response was patronizing, and a full-fledged battle ensued around me as I sat there feeling a bit woozy and slightly bewildered, still pleasantly dazed and lost in the fading buzz of the anaesthetic.

Once home, my mother, still fuming, turned to me and said, 'You don't have to go to school tomorrow if you don't want. I understand that you might not feel very good about the way your teeth look.' We looked straight at each other. Something had just happened, but I wasn't sure what. All I'd ever wanted was to be left alone and allowed to stay at home. I had spent a great deal of energy trying to convince her that I had to stay at home because of some counterfeit physical ailment, but all of a sudden it wasn't what I wanted at all.

She stood over me there in the living room, the cats howling for their dinner because we'd returned home so late from the hospital, and offered me, what, compassion? The more I think of it now I'm certain her offer to stay at home was an attempt to understand what she must have known instinctively. But it was too late. I'd already given up that fight. I'd already begun to believe what the boys at school told me. I understood my mother's offer only as barbed verification of what I trusted to be the indisputable truth: I was too ugly to go to school. I virtually stopped going to the seventh grade, but was moved along with everybody else to the eighth. My grades were only mediocre, and my passing surely had to do more with ineptitude on the school's part than any true academic accomplishment on mine.

I relished that summer as no other. My friend Jan and I took our infatuation with horses to ridiculous proportions. We spent all of our play time pretending we were horses, galloping around her yard, jumping over whatever obstacle we could set up. Whoever got round the best was given a home-made blue ribbon, and afterward we would kneel on her lawn and dare each other to graze, the curiously familiar and sweet flavour of grass filling our mouths and turning our front teeth green.

Jan's parents were paying for her to take riding lessons that summer and I was filled with envy. We couldn't afford them. Sometimes she'd invite me to go with her and I would, though I hated the superior tone she took with me then. I went anyway because the very presence of horses overwhelmed me, filled my whole body with a sensation so physical and complete that I'd be transported during those hours. I did nothing but fear the passing of each moment sitting by the fence watching Jan ride, because I knew that each moment was finite, that eventually we'd have to go home and all I would have left would be the wonderful, peaty smell on my palms to remind me of the horses. Jan started boasting that her parents were going to buy her a horse, that they'd build a stable for it in the empty field by the lake and that, maybe, just maybe, she'd let me come and help her take care of it. We spent long afternoons thinking up names for the horse, though according to my taste, her ideas were sentimental, unoriginal choices such as Beauty, or Black.

Jan never actually got her horse, but that June shortly after my fourteenth birthday I got my job as stable hand at Diamond E. It was the perfect environment for me. The other hands were generally a couple of years older than me, mostly girls but also two boys, Sean and Ray. The girls were nice enough to me and eventually became my friends, though I never felt completely free with them, completely at ease. We came from different worlds. They were raucous and wild and I loved them for this. Epithets the likes of which I've never heard even from my own wild brothers flew from everyone's lips, and there was a glorious delight in getting as muddy and dirty as possible. When I came home at the end of the day my mother always made me undress in the garage. I was proud of the mud all over me and the tired ache from trying to hoist bales of hay, however ineffectually. As the summer wore on I got tanned and gained weight and grew physically stronger every day.

I loved the basic needs of the animals, how they had to be fed and watered no matter how tired or hot or late you were. There was a primacy to it, a simplicity I recognized from coping with the pain of my treatments, a shedding of all extraneous grievances to reveal a purely physical core, a meaning which did not extend beyond the confines of one's body. When feeding time was near, a pandemonium broke out among the horses, filling the barn with neighing and kicking and squealing. And just as suddenly, as soon as our work of dragging buckets and hauling hay was over, a peace descended. It was a quiet filled with chewing sounds and soft snorts and a sense of rest which felt ancient and good. Sometimes, late at night when I couldn't sleep, I would call the stable, knowing no one was there, and imagine the sound of the phone echoing in the horse-filled barn.

I kept my new world with both its physical pleasures and new social experiences completely separated from my family, who did not seem particularly interested anyway, though they were certainly glad I'd found something 'healthy' to do with my time. School was coming around again and I actually looked forward to returning only because of the barn. Horse-fever is common among junior high-school girls and I thought that my new position might aid my status at school. Back at the barn everyone else was preparing to return to school as well, including Jeanne, who was boy crazy and had a crush on Sean.

The day before school we were all sitting on top of the hay pile, a group of some six girls with Jeanne standing on top, pointing to each person and asking, 'If Sean asked you out, would you go with him?' The group of girls were mixed in ages and in physical development, Jeanne being the oldest at sixteen. Alison and I were the youngest at fourteen. Alison actually looked fourteen whereas I, with my body still reeling from the effects of all the chemotherapy and puberty still a whole year away, looked about ten. Jeanne seemed to be asking everyone systematically, but she wasn't actually thinking of asking me. Sean would never ask me out, it was a completely ridiculous question, and the thought that we all might have acknowledged this fact together seemed worse than anything else in the whole world.

Finally, the moment of truth came, everyone else had been asked. Jeanne turned to me and, only because she didn't know how else *not* to leave me out, asked the question. I hesitated, not sure how to respond, but then Chris came to my aid and answered for me. 'Why would Sean want to go out with her?' 'Well, I'm just asking,' Jeanne replied. I shifted uncomfortably on the hay, glad Chris had spoken for me. This was the moment when I knew definitively that I would never have a boyfriend, that no one would ever be interested in me in that way. I suppose I had learned this already from the boys at school, but never had I actually formed the inner sentence, expressed it in actual terms to myself.

Because I was never going to have love (a realization too painful to linger over, I embraced it swiftly and finally), I cast myself in the role of Hero of Love. No longer in terms of proving my worth on the chemotherapy table, I would become a hero in a new sense of the word: through my understanding of the real beauty that existed in the world. I suspected that it was my very ugliness which allowed me access to this other beauty. My face may have closed the door on love and beauty in their fleeting states, but didn't my face also open me up to perceptions I might otherwise be blind to? At the end of each day as I lay in the bathtub, I looked at my child's body, utterly unlike a woman's. I considered the desire to have it develop into a woman's body a weakness, a straying from my chosen path of truth. And as I lay in bed at night, I considered my powers, my heightened sense of self-awareness, feeling not as if I had chosen this path, but that it had been chosen for me.

Beauty had nothing to do with the ephemeral world of boys, of this I felt sure. This was driven home to me ever more when junior high school started up again and I watched as my sister and her friends began their own puberty. They put on blue eye shadow, blow-dried their hair, and spent interminably long hours at the local mall. My own notions of what made a woman beautiful were more classically oriented: if I could look like anyone in the world it would be either Marlene Dietrich or Botticelli's Venus. I definitely did *not* aspire to look like Farrah Fawcett, of this much I was sure. I looked at girls in my class, their perfect faces, and wondered why on earth they ruined them with so much make-up, such stupid hair. If *I* had a face like that, I'd tell myself, then harshly reprimand myself for any stirrings of desire. My face was my face and it was stupid to wish it any other way.

At school the gang of boys from last year appeared to have dispersed and I was free to eat in the lunch room again, but a new group had formed and they tracked me down relentlessly every day between fourth and fifth periods when I was going from gym to English class, which were at opposite ends of the school. By the time I reached the staircase near my English classroom nearly everyone else was already there, leaving me to climb these stairs alone, free from the crowds. Alone, that is, until a group of about six boys discovered they could reliably find me in this stairwell each day at the same time, and took to waiting for me. Their teasing was the most hurtful of all because it wasn't even directed at me, but at a boy named Jerry.

'Hey look, it's Jerry's girlfriend. Hey Jerry, go on, ask your girlfriend out.' I heard Jerry meekly protest, but I knew that he was as much at their mercy as I was, and I knew that to have me called his girlfriend was just about the most malicious insult the other boys could level at him. I even went so far as to feel sorry for Jerry, though I never even saw him as I refused to lift my gaze up from the floor. What morons, I thought to myself, what misguided morons. I wanted to hate them. But what I knew of hate had already taught me that it was just a barrier to another type of feeling.

Martin Luther King was one of my heroes, and he had said, 'I will not allow my oppressors to dictate to me the means of my resistance.' That seemed like a far truer thing, a far deeper thing. I wanted to hate them, but instead I tried to forgive them. I thought that if I could do this, the pain they caused would be extinguished. Though I had genuine glimpses of what charity and transcendence meant, I was shooting for nothing less than sainthood, and more often, it worked out that after my daily meeting with them, I ended up hating myself instead.

The horses remained my one real source of relief. When I was in their presence, nothing else mattered. Animals were both the lives I took care of and the lives who took care of me. Horses neither disapproved nor approved of what I looked like, it was only how I treated them that counted, how my actions weighted themselves in the world. I loved to stand next to them with no other humans in sight and rest my head against their warm flanks, trace the whorls in their hide with the fingers of one hand while the other hand rested on the soft skin between their legs. All the while, I'd listen to the patient sounds of their stomachs and smell the sweet air from their lungs as attentively as if I were being sent information from another world.

In the middle of the school year, several months before my fifteenth birthday, I went to see Dr John Conley again, the surgeon who had removed my jaw, to discuss plans for reconstructing it. I had known all along that something was going to be done to 'fix' my face, but up until this point I don't think I really believed it.

It was strange being back in Dr Conley's office again. To be in a doctor's office without the threat of chemo or dental work seemed so simple and easy. As he examined me, he held my head in his hands, touching my face as no else had in years. It was only then that I realized how guarded I had become about my face; simply relaxing and allowing him to touch me there was akin to surrender, and the closest I ever got to experiencing trust. After the examination, he sat down and spoke to me in the tone of someone speaking to a child, which served to both instantly destroy and strangely build the trust I had felt with him only moments before.

He explained that the biggest problem would come from all the radiation treatment. Irradiated tissue tended not to take grafts too well, and also presented a higher rate of reabsorption, meaning that even if the graft wasn't actually rejected, it might simply be 'taken back' by my body and shrink back down to nothing. He proposed a technique which required the use of pedestals, and which would necessitate several operations. In the first operation, two parallel incisions would be made into my stomach. The strip of skin between these incisions would be lifted up and rolled into a sort of tube, a seam running alongside it where the two incisions would be sewn together, with both ends of the tube still attached to my stomach, resembling a kind of handle: this handle was the pedestal. Six weeks after that, one end of the handle would be cut from my stomach and attached to my wrist, so that my hand would be literally sewn to my stomach for six weeks. Then, the end of the tube which was still attached to my stomach would be severed and then that end would be sewn to my face, so that now my hand would be attached to my face. Six weeks after that, my hand would be cut loose and the pedestal, or flap as they called it, would be nestled completely into the gap created by my missing jaw. This would only be the first pedestal: it would take several, plus additional operations to carve everything into a recognizable shape. It would probably take about ten years, altogether. Ten years! I was horrified. I would be twenty-five years old in ten years: ancient. Did I have to devote the next ten years of my life to one surgery after another? Ten years; my God.

I was crushed. It must have shown because Dr Conley started explaining how I shouldn't worry about how I looked, how everyone had something they didn't like about their face. Why, he himself had terrible acne as a teenager, and that had made him feel awful. Acne, was he serious? How could my problem actually be compared to acne? Any hope I'd allowed myself died right then.

My despair worsened a few days later when I went to the library with my father. While he stayed downstairs and picked amongst the fiction, I went upstairs to the non-fiction department and secretly looked up books on plastic surgery. In the middle of giant, out-dated tomes, I found photographs of the pedestal procedure. The people in the photographs looked like freaks. The way their own skin and muscle were sewn to disjointed parts of their anatomy looked like illustrations of some brilliant medieval torture device. Worst of all, the final outcome looked exactly like what they were: people with alien bits of flesh sewn onto them. To my eye, many of the people used as examples looked even worse afterwards. I was so frightened my breath literally would not come, and I had to sit down with my head between my legs until the buzzing was gone from my ears. Was this what my life was going to be? I felt utterly without hope, utterly alone and without any chance of anyone ever loving me. Feeling as if I had uncovered some horrible secret, I went downstairs for my father.

As we drove home together, he asked me what was wrong, but I was incapable of telling him anything. Back at home I went to my room where I wanted desperately to cry, but even the tears were numbed back. I lay frozen on my bed watching a spider walking back and forth on my ceiling until my mother called me for dinner. For the very first time, I wished that I were dead.

Relief came in two unexpected ways. The first occurred some months later, towards summer and the end of the eighth grade, when Kelly, a girl I had met at the barn, had to move to another state. Unable to take her horse, an ex-racehorse named Sure Swinger, she arranged it with my parents to give him to me. I'd never understood just how quickly, how splendidly and suddenly reality could change, how you could look down at the shoes on your own two feet and wonder if they, too, were real. The second form of comfort came in the person of Dr Daniel Baker, a younger associate of Dr Conley's. He and some other doctors were working on a technique involving microsurgery, a very new field at the time, to graft vascularized free-flaps.

This 'state of the art' reconstructive surgery involved taking a large chunk of soft tissue, probably from my groin, and in one fell swoop sewing the whole thing, veins and all, onto the jaw area. This not only dispensed with the cumbersome, multi-staged procedure of the pedestals, but it also offered a greater chance of graft survival because the new tissue would have its own blood supply. Dr Baker explained that it was best to wait another year or so, perhaps until I was sixteen, so that I could get some more growing in first. A major operation followed by lesser ones to shape the graft would be required, but Dr Baker seemed to think there was a good chance of achieving 'a near-normal jaw-line.' I can still picture my father's reaction as he stood in the corner of Dr Baker's office, listening to his words, beaming. I had never mentioned my fears concerning my face to my father, and in my solipsism it had never occurred to me that he, too, shared my unhappiness. The literal halo of joy which surrounded him now was a revelation to me. His joy made me feel better, though it also occurred to me that my face must really be as bad as I feared if he also found such relief at the possibility of this surgery.

Maybe life was going to be alright, after all. Maybe there was a chance that this wasn't my actual face at all, but the face of some interloper, some ugly intruder, and in reality my 'real' face, the one I was meant to have all along, was within reach. I began to imagine my 'original face', the one free from all deviation, from all error. I believed that if none of this had happened to me, I would have been beautiful. I looked in the mirror closely and imagined the lower half of my face filled out, normal. Reaching my hand up, I covered my chin and jaw and yes, even I could see that the rest of my face really was beautiful. As soon as I took my hand away it seemed to me that the ugliness of the lower half cancelled out the upper half, but now this didn't matter so much to me: it was all going to be 'fixed'.

What would it be like simply to walk down the street and trust that no one would say anything nasty to me? My only clues were from Halloween, and during the winter when I could wrap up the lower half of my face in a scarf and talk to people who had no idea of how the beauty of the upper half of my face was actually a lie, a trick that would be exposed the minute I had to take off the scarf. To feel that confidence without that threat of exposure, how could I possibly want anything more? Because if someone thought I were beautiful, and here I could almost not dare to think such a thing, then they might even love me. Me, as an individual, as a person.

I'd been rationalizing my own desires for so long that I was genuinely perplexed as to whether or not this sudden and glorious sense of relief at the prospect of having my face fixed was valid or not. Was the love that I'd been guarded against for so long going to be the genuine reward for my suffering? I had put a great deal of effort into accepting that my life would be one without love and beauty in order to be comforted by Love and Beauty. Did my eager willingness to grasp onto the idea of 'fixing' my face somehow invalidate all those years of toil? I simply did not trust the idea that happiness could be an option.

For a few months I settled into a routine of living what felt like three separate lives. Days were filled with school, where I tried to be as fiercely intelligent as I could. My armour would become my academic prowess from which I was developing a superiority complex as earnestly built as it was defensively acquired. In my second life I still lived in a violent fantasy in which I had no choice but to appreciate the life I led in reality, the one in which my face seemed a frivolous thing compared with a landmine or a pogrom. The third life took place after school, and all day during the summer, when I went to my horse, with whom I was conducting nothing less than a romantic relationship.

I knew his whole being. There was not one part of his body I could not touch, not one part of his personality I did not know at least as well as my own. When we went on long rides through the woods I would tell him everything I knew, and then explain to him why I loved him so much, why he was special from other horses, how I would take care of him for the rest of his life, how I would never leave him or let anyone harm him. After the ride, I would take him to graze in an empty field where I would lie down on his broad bare back and think I was the luckiest girl alive, his weight shifting beneath me as he moved towards the next bite of grass. Sometimes I took him to the stream and laughed as he pawed at the water, screaming in delight when he tried to lie down in it. Best of all was when I happened to find him lying down in his stall. Carefully, so as not to spook him, I'd creep in and lie down on top of his giant body, his great animal heat and breath rising up to swallow my own smaller heat and less substantial air.

9
World of Unknowing

SCHOOL STARTED AGAIN, and in my ninth grade English class we began reading poetry. For our first assignment, we were to read Theodore Roethke's 'My Papa's Waltz'. I read it dutifully the night before and recognized in the image of the father's dirty hand and the boy's dizzying bewilderment something beautiful and important, something that vaguely had to do with my own family. And as I recognized myself, I also realized the precision of language, that the poem could not have been written in any other way except exactly as it had been. I also suspected that the poem's power over me was from its unassailable ability to say exactly what it was that felt so right and true. I think I already understood that beauty was somehow related to mystery, but this was the first time I ever saw that mystery was not just a cause, but also a natural result of beauty. I tried to say all this in class the next day, but my teacher just wanted us to answer the question of whether or not the boy loved his father. We spent the forty minutes debating along those lines as what I knew about my own love for my father seemed to grow only more distant and closed off to me.

When my father used to come home late at night, he would shout greetings to everybody as he came through the door, and Sarah and the dogs and I would go running to greet him. But as we were getting older we seemed less interested in this ritual, and it got so that only the dogs would actually get up to greet him, while Sarah and I tossed off distracted greetings from our seats in front of the television set. One evening, I had a terrible premonition of the day when he would come home after Sarah and I had grown up and moved out and the dogs were long dead, and there would only be his own voice echoing emptily up the stairs. I felt a strange chill, a hollow and unspeakably sad chill, almost as if I had seen a ghost. From that day on I made a point, even when I didn't particularly feel like it, of greeting him at the top of the stairs. I saw it only in terms of how I would one day be absent from his life: it never occurred to me that he would ever be absent from mine.

Before my father's death, just seven or eight months after my premonition, I was to experience another death. Only four months after I had received him, Swinger developed an infection in his hoof. I watched carefully as Gene, one of the only regular adult employees at the stable, gave Swinger the prescribed penicillin injection in his neck. Then I went down to the tack room to put something away. After I'd finished my chore, I turned back to the ring where Gene was leading Swinger. I was about to crack a joke like, 'What do you think you're doing with my horse?' when I realized something was terribly wrong. Swinger was in the process of falling down and trying to get back up, only to fall down again. Finally he could not get back up at all. A crowd had formed and everyone was yelling and shouting and trying to rouse him, but his legs were sticking almost straight out and trembling and his eyes were rolling into the back of his head. Gene shouted at me to run and get a blanket from the barn. I tore away and fumbled to get the blanket off its rack. Once I had it in hand, I ran back to the ring but as I got closer I saw everyone was just standing there, no more shouting, and as I neared the gate Gene got there before me. With one arm, he held it shut and wouldn't let me back in. I looked at him, dropped the blanket and burst into tears, all the while strangely aware of the melodrama of it all, as if I remembered this scene from a movie I'd already seen. The shot was of Gene's strong and hairy arm barring my way, of everyone standing so silent, of Swinger's huge dark body on the ground. Although I had never liked Gene very much, I allowed him to hold me as I sobbed. I smelled the sweat on his clothes and looked towards Swinger and saw the slow line of urine seeping into the lightly coloured dust. I had read that you peed and defecated when you died, and now I knew it was true.

I couldn't bring myself to call my mother to tell her what had happened and asked someone else to call for me. She came to pick me up and for some reason I was frightened by the prospect of her reaction: would she be mad? Naturally, she was very sympathetic, but I couldn't shake the feeling of shame. When we got home I went wordlessly down to my room and watched television in a stupor of grief. Finally I heard my father come home, shout his usual greeting, and walk up the stairs into the kitchen which was above my room. I could hear my parents' footsteps above me and I knew she was telling him. I listened as he walked down the stairs, then silence for a moment as he walked over the thick rug towards my room. I felt the same sense of shame I'd experienced with my mother, not unlike the times he'd visited me in the hospital. He offered his condolences and kissed my ears, which tickled and annoyed me so that I pushed him away, and then left. My mourning was so untouchable that I had no clue as to what to do with it. Perhaps Swinger had died because I loved him too much: what other reason could there be? Why else would God allow the being I loved more than any other living thing in the world, including myself, to die like that? If there was some kind of meaning to this, some lesson I was supposed to learn, I didn't care. Ever since the moment that Gene had stopped me at the gate, I had been unable to stop observing everything from an untraceable distance. Even as I felt the worst pain I could ever remember feeling, a dramatic sense of my situation crept in and there, in front of my private audience, I played my role of the hapless and ill-fated lover once again.

While I was stricken over Swinger's death for several months, time did eventually perform its healing task and gradually I became excited at the prospect of getting another horse, which my parents promised me. I knew that money was still an issue and that this new horse might not materialize straight away, but I knew that they would not go back on their word. Then, sometime after Christmas, my mother received a phone call from my dad's boss, explaining that he was in the hospital because of stomach pains. My first reaction was that this would put a wrench in my new-horse plans. My mother was certain he was only being a hypochondriac, that it was nothing at all. Maybe it was his ulcer acting up again and he was just overreacting. But he was still in the hospital the next day, they were keeping him for tests, and he was still in the day after that, and the next day, too. My mother started visiting him every day, yet the rest of us stayed behind, assuming he would be out the very next day.

The weeks turned into months and each day we received a new report on my father's health. He had pancreatitis: no one would say if he would get better or not. One day, towards the end of March, my mother came home and told us they'd put my father on oxygen. Inwardly, I shuddered. Everything I knew about hospitals told me that this was a bad thing. My father was going to die, and as bad as this knowledge was, it was made worse by my notion that I was the only one who understood this. My family was not the sort to discuss things openly. Though we all must have been hurting, we did not speak of my father except with a forced optimism.

Just before my father went into the hospital, he'd bought an expensive hand-tailored suit, and he'd also joined a record club that began sending the complete sets of Beethoven's works. The fancy suit that he'd been so proud of, which was also the source of a fight between him and my mother because of its price, hung unworn in his closet. And each week a new selection of records arrived, wrapped in plastic, which we piled unopened next to the phonograph in the living room. My father's bedroom was a disaster area, filled with stray papers and dirty socks and odd cups and occasional forks. I went in and surveyed it all just as I'd done when I was younger and he was away at work, but now I was looking for something else. I had no idea what. Before, I'd wanted some kind of clue as to what it was to be my father, what it was to be a man, to be an adult. Now I was looking for something which would explain my father's life to me. I couldn't find it.

Back in the living room, I could no longer take the sight of the unopened records any more. Ripping the plastic off them, I sat down in front of the record player and in the course of five or six hours listened to only a fraction of Beethoven's complete works. I wanted to see why he loved Beethoven so much. Finally, I fell asleep lying there on the carpet and was awakened by the dogs barking at my mother's return. Hurriedly, I put the records away. I'm not sure why, but I didn't want anyone to know I'd listened to them.

The whole time he was in the hospital, I only went to visit my father once. Even after all these years, I don't understand why we stayed away. Were we just so adrift in our own sea of grief that we were able to convince ourselves that it was better this way? He grew more and more disorientated. My mother reported back that he kept pointing to a pin she wore, a pin he'd bought for her before they were married, pointing to it as if he were picking it out again, for the first time. He became paranoid, talking about Germans and the dogs the Germans had set on him when he was a prisoner of war during the Second World War. He'd been a pilot in the RAF and we had a dashing, fuzzy picture of him in his flak suit, smiling at an unseen person casting a shadow near his feet. It was easy to forget about that part of my father's life because he never spoke of it. Once I remember watching 'Hogan's Heroes' while he was in the room. He was appalled that a television comedy would be set in a German war camp. Knowing nothing of his war experience at the time, I told him I thought he was overreacting. It pained me to think that now, near the end of his life, he was reliving this nightmare, as alone as he had been the first time. We spent the next couple of weeks waiting. Every time the phone rang, everyone in the whole house went silent.

I was dreading this inevitable phone call, but mostly because I did not want to see the rest of my family's reaction to it. I knew that Sarah would break down and cry, but I had no idea what everyone else would do. I wanted my father to die and for there to be no fuss, no outbreaks, no displays. I was terrified. When the call did come, at last, one afternoon some six weeks before my sixteenth birthday, my mother was on the phone at the far end of the kitchen, my brother Nicholas was sitting at one end of the table, Sarah was sitting at the other end, and I was standing in the doorway. Susie was away at college and Sean was living in California. Sarah, Nicholas and I remained motionless as we listened to my mother speak, thanking the doctor for all he had done, and when she got off she told us matter-of-factly and very sadly what we already knew. To my great surprise, it wasn't Sarah who cried, but Nicholas. He put his head down on the table and wept and all I could think of was how I didn't expect this, just as I didn't expect Sarah to sit there so calmly, and I turned my head and looked at the painting on the wall next to me. It was a head of Christ painted by Sean, one I'd passed several thousand times, yet I felt I was seeing it for the first time. I'd never noticed how much brown he'd used in the thorns, how much gold for the skin. It all seemed so very odd, so very distant, and I was reminded how clearly I'd seen the ceiling in Dr Woolf's office that last day there. Was this feeling that everything was happening for the first time real, did grief heighten vision, or was it only an illusion, a way to distance myself from what was happening?

Along with sadness, a sense of relief followed my father's death. At least we weren't waiting any more. Also, it seemed we were going to be getting some money from the insurance company, and the prospect of paying off some bills and finally getting ahead offered a guilty sense of pleasure. I was sitting in the kitchen a couple of days after my dad's funeral. Perhaps we were still in shock, but Sarah and I were laughing hysterically over a new joke we'd heard, and just as we were in the thick of it, the phone rang. It was my surgeon, Dr Baker. I was shocked to hear his voice, for he was nothing less than a monumental figure in my life, but when he offered his condolences, all I could do was jauntily reply, as if he'd just apologized for stepping on my shoe. 'Oh, that's alright, it doesn't matter.' As soon as I hung up the phone I realized what I'd just done. But as I told Sarah what had just happened, the two of us started up again in our uncontrollable laughter.

That June, a few weeks after my sixteenth birthday, I went into New York University Medical Center for my first reconstructive operation, my first micro-vascularized free-flap. I liked this hospital: it was newer and better staffed and I was no longer relegated to the children's ward. This new ward was devoted solely to plastic surgery, and I was shocked to see how many people were there getting their noses done, their faces lifted. The woman in the room next to me was having her breast reconstructed after a mastectomy, and she insisted on telling me all about her own scars, her own feelings of ugliness. I was in no position to listen: her face was beautiful and she had a husband who brought her a dozen red roses. It was true she was missing a breast, but I didn't see how that mattered as long as she had these other things. No one could see her missing breast when she walked down the street, no one would make fun of her or think she was ugly, and she had someone who loved her. I listened to her and I saw that she was genuinely suffering, that her feelings of ugliness consumed her as much as mine consumed me, but she was mistaken, I thought, for there was no doubt she was beautiful. Her problems lay in her perception. Talking with her only convinced me more of how important it was in this world to have a beautiful face. Still, I liked her, and I liked being treated as an adult by another adult. We ordered out for Chinese food for what I kept calling 'my last meal'. 'No, no, don't say that,' she tried to reassure me. I just couldn't get her to see that I was joking, and I could tell she was new at this hospital stuff.

The anaesthetist came to see me that night and decided that I might be hard to intubate (the process of having a breathing tube inserted into my windpipe), and so he would do it while I was awake. It didn't sound like a big deal, and I didn't think twice about it.

The next morning, however, as I lay dazed on the stretcher I heard them talking about nasal intubation. Immediately I started worrying, and for good reason. First, they tried passing a tube up one nostril. It didn't hurt, but when it reached the back of my throat I gagged. Worse, they kept prying my mouth open to see where it was going. They couldn't get it, so they pulled it out and tried the other nostril. By now I was upset, but I lay as still as I could. That nostril didn't work either, so they decided to go straight through my mouth. This required prising it open and keeping it open, which hurt like hell, but worse was that at each attempt to pass the tube, my airway was temporarily blocked and I couldn't breathe, which put me into a panic. The pre-op medications were slowing my reactions and making it hard for me to understand what was going on. I instinctively started to struggle, reaching up and trying to push their strangling hands away from me. Two nurses came and held me down and I started to cry and struggle even more, but they only held me down tighter and kept pushing the tube down my throat. They must have sedated me even further because my reactions grew even more sluggish and all reality ceased to exist outside the six foot-long confines of that stretcher. I begged them to stop, but no one responded. This upset me most of all. No one cared, or seemed to, and I wailed even louder. Then, they must have succeeded, because suddenly everyone seemed to disappear and I was left lying in peace, floating, but still crying hard. I looked up and there was Dr Baker, looking down at me. He reached out his hand and, in an exact replication of the gesture I'd received during my very first operation, placed it on my forehead. I was calmed instantaneously, as if all my sorrows existed within that one single point on my forehead. I remember a surreal vision of myself as if I were a bystander in the room, looking at the clownish cap they'd made me wear to hold back my hair, the clear, greenish tube arching awkwardly out of my mouth, and then I was asleep.

When I awoke I was in a lot of pain, but it was pain in my hip, where the graft had come from, far away from my face, my 'self', so it was easier to deal with. As soon as I remembered why I'd had an operation, I reached up to touch my face. There was a large, warm and very soft mass where there used to be an indent. I felt a complicated trail of stitches, and near my ear was a drain. Turning my head, I tried to get a glimpse of myself in the reflection of the metal bed-rails, but could only glimpse a distorted image of something I didn't readily recognize as my own face. When my mother came to visit she asked how I felt and I responded with a question.

'What does it look like?'

'Well, dear, it's a bit hard to tell. It's very swollen.'

'But do you think it will be alright?'

'Well, he's definitely filled it out. But it's so swollen now, you have to wait and see.'

I didn't want to wait. After she was gone I asked a nurse to describe it to me. 'You have to understand that it's very swollen and bruised. It will change.' I asked for a mirror. Sitting up was too painful, so I lay there and held it above me, staring up at someone I only vaguely recognized. Swollen was an understatement. This new thing on my face was huge, almost touching my collar bone. What repulsed me most of all was a large strip of foreign skin, much paler than my facial skin, running along the lower half of the graft. This was surrounded by dozens of minute stitches and it looked just like what it was, a patch. The rest of my face looked horrible as well, all pale and puffy, and my hair was full of dried blood. I handed the mirror back to the nurse, thanked her, and went back to sleep. When I woke up again I tried not to think about my face, I tried to remind myself that everything they said was true, it had only been a matter of hours since the surgery was finished and I couldn't judge the end result by what I had seen in the mirror. There would be more operations to revise the graft, to remove the extra skin, which had been purposefully placed there to allow for all the swelling, and to allow for better monitoring of the underlying graft. The next few hours were crucial, and it was important that the graft keep its blood supply. Every hour, a nurse walked in and touched me there, to feel its warmth, and then poked me, to test capillary reaction. I saw their hands coming near my face, but I couldn't feel a thing. I wasn't in the least bit concerned with whether or not the graft would survive, I was simply assuming it would. Far more important to me was whether or not all this had been some horrible mistake in the first place. I knew better than to expect perfection, yet I had not quite anticipated how *foreign* it would look. I shut down, I tried not to think about it. When I did think about it, I projected my thinking forward, to the next operation, the one which would fix this one.

I turned my attention to the actual process of healing. At first lying still had been no problem, but now I was getting cramps in my legs. Yet, in order to relieve the cramps I had to move my legs, and that sent shooting pains through the muscles in my torso. I felt as if I were in some kind of science fiction movie, one where people are kept prisoner within bizarre, invisible force-fields. At the same time, I didn't really mind the pain. Pain, if nothing else, was honest and open and you knew exactly what you were dealing with.

After the first few hours I was taken out of Intensive Care and sent to Special Care, which was one rung lower on the attention scale. There were three other beds. The one directly across from me was empty. In the one next to that, kitty-corner from my bed, was a girl who, I found out from eavesdropping, was in the process of dying from a brain tumour. Relatives came and gave her presents which she opened with a blank, unknowing face, and when she spoke it was unintelligible. She would grow frustrated when no one understood her and would throw a tantrum, sending objects flying across the room and towards the bed next to mine, where a teenage boy named Michael was recovering.

Michael's first comment to me was about my stuffed Kangaroo, which my mother had bought for me and which all the nurses commented on. He said, dryly, that my Kangaroo had usurped his monkey as the cutest toy on the ward. His monkey hung from a bar at arm's length above his bed. I didn't know what usurped meant, and when I asked him he laughed. He was only a year older than me, but he seemed to have lived a whole life already.

Michael would reach up to the bar hanging over his bed and use his arms to hoist himself up. He didn't wear a pyjama top, so that when his back was momentarily off the bed, I could see his muscles flex and the red lines indented into the pale skin of his back from lying on the sheets too long. He told me he'd dived off the top of a two-storey building into a pool and had hurt his back. 'Why'd you do that?' 'I don't know,' he answered, looking up at the ceiling. 'It was a friend's pool,' he said again after a moment, as if that should somehow clarify the situation.

Whenever he spoke, he always sounded slightly bored, slightly distant. But whenever he talked with me, which was quite a bit over the next couple of days, I always felt privileged that he was speaking to me at all. If he were one of the boys at school, would he be among those who made fun of me? I stole sideways glances at him, his long wavy hair, the stubble on his chin and upper lip and thought that, probably, yes, he would be. Yet here we were lying next to each other, both of us in a lot of pain, and I knew that here he would never dream of saying anything mean to me. Faintly, I felt slightly triumphant. Someone from 'that other world' had come over to mine.

One night Michael refused to take a particular pill, and the doctor had come to argue with him about it. Michael fought with the doctors all the time, always questioning them and refusing to do things he didn't want to do; he was my complete opposite, as I still looked for praise as 'a model patient'. It was in the middle of the night and the main overhead lights were off. His curtain was drawn and I saw Michael and the doctor's shadows thrown against the yellow curtain. The pill Michael was refusing to take was something he needed for his stomach. The doctor was explaining how when someone spent so much time lying down, it fooled with your digestive juices, and this pill would counteract that. Michael kept refusing, his voice rising in protest, which I didn't understand at all. Why didn't he just take it? Then, inexplicably, he started crying and screamed at the doctor to leave.

As the doctor left, I lay there, looking at Michael's shadow, wondering if I should say something.

A few minutes later, a nurse came to empty out his urine catheter bag. I knew he had one, I had one too, but I'd never really thought about how it might work with a man. The nurse didn't close the curtain properly, and when I looked over I saw for the first time an adult male's penis, this one being pushed up and held falsely erect by the tube inserted into it. It came as a shock because it was the first time I acknowledged that Michael was permanently paralyzed, at the age of seventeen, all because of a stupid trick that took him ten seconds to perform.

I couldn't help but compare his situation to my own. My life was 'different' from most people's, but it was essentially my own. I hated the face I remembered having a few days ago, and I knew nothing of the face I had now except that I feared it. But, it existed. It was there, and I had only to look at it to know what it was. Michael had lost something he was never going to get back: my face had only changed into the next shape it was meant to be. I could not dare to think that the next shape was something I might actually want, or like, but I had a sudden sense that to have it at all meant something.

Two days later I was transferred onto a regular ward, and as I was wheeled away I promised Michael I would come and visit him, but I never did. As soon as I was back on the ward, filled with nose jobs and jowl tucks, I grew fearful of my distorted face again, and put Michael and his predicament out of my mind. I was walking to the bathroom by myself now, and each time I opened the door the first thing I saw was my own face reflected back at me. Was that really me? I knew it had to be, but how could it possibly relate to the person I thought I was, or wanted to be? I considered the whole operation a failure, and when the doctors came round and told me how well it was healing, how good it looked, my heart sank. We were speaking two different languages, and if this looked good, then what I thought looked good must be an impossible dream. I felt stupid for having had any expectations or hopes at all.

When I got home, I thought of Michael again and again. Did he ever re-imagine himself standing on top of that roof, trying to remember what it was like not to know his fate for just one split second longer? If he didn't, I did it for him. I'd close my eyes in order to feel the height, see the bright blue of the pool winking below me, bend my legs and feel the pull in my calves as I jumped up and then down, falling from one world of unknowing into the next one of perpetual regret.

10

The Habits of Self-Consciousness

IT WAS ONLY when I got home from the hospital that I permitted myself to look more closely at my new face. It was still extremely swollen, it would be months before it went down, and there was a long thin scar running the length of it. In the middle of the scar was an island of pale skin which had come from my hip. This skin, I was reassured, would be taken away in a later operation; it was only there so that the other skin on my face wouldn't be pulled too tight from the swelling. Placing my hand over the swollen and discoloured parts, I tried to imagine how it might look once it was 'better'. If I positioned the angle of my face, the angle of my hand and the angle of the mirror all just right, it looked okay. Actually, in my mind, it looked even better than okay, it looked beautiful. But it was a beauty which existed in the future, and even then, only a possible future. As it was, I hated my face. I turned my thoughts inward again, and this strange fantasy of beauty became something very private, a wish I would have been ashamed to let anyone in on. Primarily, it was a fantasy of relief. Every time I tried to imagine what it would be like to be beautiful, I could only imagine living without the perpetual fear of being alone, with the great burden of isolation, which is what I felt when I felt ugly, being lifted from me.

The beginning of High School was a couple of months away, and each day I checked my face in private, wondering what I would look like by my first day at a new school. I thought I would have had a second 'revising' operation by the time school started, but as it turned out I would have to wait at least another three months, a span of time which seemed useless and insurmountable to me. What was the whole point, if I still had to walk into school that first day looking like this?

128

There was only one solution, as far as I could work out, and that was to stop caring. I became pretentious. I picked out books to read that were thick and had Russian names, and I carted them around with me. Sometimes I even read them. *Anna Karenina, The Brothers Karamazov, Dead Souls.* I also read *Jude the Obscure* simply because I liked the title, and anything else that sounded difficult and deep. Often, I missed the subtle nuances of these books, but they presented me with a version of the world where honour and virtue and dedication to the truth counted. These stories comforted me even though it didn't escape my attention that these qualities were primarily ascribed to men. The women might be virtuous as well, but their physical beauty seemed crucial to the story.

The first day of school finally came. I took the bus, entered my strange home-room, and went through my day of classes as invisibly as possible. By now my hair was long, reaching down past my shoulders, and I walked around with my head bent, my dark blonde hair covering half my face. Having divested myself of seeking anything as inconsequential as social status, I spent the days observing my peers with my perfectly calibrated air of disinterest. I remained the outsider, just like so many of the characters I had read about, and in this role I found great comfort. Doubtless, I was more keenly aware of the subtleties involved in the various dramas and social dances of my classmates than they were themselves.

For the most part, I was left alone. People were a bit more mature and it was rare that anyone openly made fun of me. But I was still poised for it. Every time I saw someone looking at me, I expected the worst. Usually, they just looked the other way and didn't register much interest one way or the other. This was fine by me, though it always seemed that just as I started to relax, to let my guard down, some loud-mouthed boy would feel a need to point out how ugly I was to his friends.

One day as I went into my English class, I found a copy of Hesse's *Siddhartha*, his own version of the story of the Buddha, lying there on my chair. My notions of Buddhism were sketchy at best, but the opening pages immediately reminded me of the same message of grace, of dignity and light that I'd first encountered in those Christian publications which had long since ceased arriving in the mail. I'd almost forgotten about my quest for enlighten-ment, how I used to spend so much time imagining my momentous meeting with the great guru. Now, after so much time and so much loss, I took it as a sign that someone had left this book on my chair. Desire and all its painful complications, I decided, was something I should and would be free of.

Two months after school started, the long-awaited revision operation was finally scheduled. I started focusing on the up-coming date, believing that perhaps my life would finally get started once I had the face I was 'supposed' to have. Logically I knew this was only one of many operations, but surely it would show promise, offer a hint of how it was all going to turn out.

After three weeks of anxiety, I went into the hospital. When I woke up in Recovery the next day I looked up to see a nurse leaning over me. She was wearing glasses. Cautiously, I looked for my reflection in them. There I was, my hair messed and my face pale and, as far as I could tell, looking exactly the same. Reaching my hand up, I felt the suture line. A few hours later when I was recovered enough to walk unaided to the bathroom, I took each careful step towards the door and geared myself up to look in the mirror. Apart from looking as if I'd just got over a bad case of the flu, I looked just the same. Even though the patch of skin was gone, the overall shape and appearance of my face was exactly the same as before.

I blamed myself for the despair I felt creeping in; it was a result of having expectations. Certainly, if this feeling was the result of too many expectations, I must guard against having any more. After all, I still had it pretty good by global standards. 'I have food,' I told myself, 'I have a place to sleep.' So what if my face was ugly, so what if other people judged me for this, that was their problem, not mine. This line of reasoning offered less consolation than it had in the past, but it distanced me from what was hurting most, and I took this as a sign that I was getting better at detaching myself from my desires.

By the morning I returned to school I had resolved that my face was actually an asset. It was true I hated it and saw it as the cause of my isolation, but in the larger scheme of things, I interpreted it as some kind of lesson. I had taught myself about reincarnation, how the soul picks its various lives with the intent of learning more and more about itself so that it might eventually break free from the cycle of karma. Why had my soul chosen this particular life, I asked myself; what was it after? What was there to learn from a face as ugly as mine? At the age of sixteen, I decided it was all about desire and love.

Over the years my perspective on 'what it was all about' has shifted, but the most important aspect then was that there *was* a reason for this happening to me. No longer feeling that I was being punished as I had during the chemo, I now undertook to see my face as an opportunity to see something that had not yet been revealed. Perhaps my face was a gift given to use towards understanding and enlightenment. This was all noble enough, except that by equating my face with ugliness, in believing that without my face I would never experience this deep, bottomless grief I called ugliness, I separated myself even further from other people, those who I thought had never experienced grief of this depth. Not that I did not allow others their own suffering. I tried my best to be empathic because I suspected it was a 'good' emotion. But in actuality I was judge and hangman, disgusted by peers who avoided their fears by putting their energy into things as insubstantial as fashion and boyfriends and gossip.

I tried my best, but for the most part I was as abysmal at seeking enlightenment as I had once been at playing dodge-ball. It didn't really seem to matter how desperately I wanted to catch that ball – I dropped it anyway. As frantically as I wanted to love everybody in the school and to waft esoterically into the ether when someone called me ugly, I was plagued with what I viewed as petty desires and secret, evil hates.

I hated Danny in my orchestra class because I had a crush on him and knew that he would never have a crush on me. Anger scared me most of all, and I repressed every stirring. Every time I felt hatred, or any other 'bad' thought, I shooed it away with a brood of spiritual truisms. But the more I tried to negate my feelings the more they reared their ugly heads. I not only harboured hatred for Danny, even while I had a crush on him, I also hated Katherine, the girl in the orchestra *he* had a crush on. Trying to repress that feeling, I found myself hating Katherine's cello, of all things, which she played exquisitely well. The cycle eventually ended with me: I hated myself for having even entertained the absurd notion that someone like Danny would like someone like me.

I didn't begrudge Danny his crush on Katherine. After all, she was pretty and talented to boot, so why shouldn't he want her? It was because I was never going to have anyone want me in that way that I mustn't desire such a thing, and in this way, I reasoned, I could be grateful to my face for 'helping' me to see the error of earthly desire. This complicated gratitude usually lasted for about five minutes before giving way to depression, plain and simple.

While there was still some insurance money from my father's death, but before we learned of the accumulated tax debt we owed, my mother generously kept her promise and bought me another horse. I kept the horse at Snowcap, a more professional and a better kept stable than Diamond E. There I undertook learning to ride seriously. My new horse had a registered name even sillier than Sure Swinger, so I simply called her Mare. I fell in love with her the same way as I had with Swinger, and I had just as bad luck with her. Not long after I got her, she broke her leg while turned out in a field. As she limped pathetically onto the trailer to be taken away, they told me they could sell her as a brood mare, but I knew she was too old for this and would be put down shortly. Again my heart had been broken, but this time I saw it in much more self-pitying terms. I told myself that anything I loved was doomed, and even as I was aware of my own overblown melodrama, just as I had been that night I nearly collapsed on the hospital floor, I was also aware of a strange comfort in this romantic, tragic role.

Luckily, the owners of Snowcap permitted me to continue on at the barn as their exercise rider. This was ideal. Not only did I get to ride all the horses I wanted for free, sometimes as many as six a day, and gain a great deal of experience in the process, but it also gave my life a centre. I withstood school all day knowing I would go straight to the barn afterward, where I would stay until eight or nine o'clock at night. The barn became the one place where I felt like myself, and I relished the physicality of riding, or performing acts I was good at, of feeling a sense of accomplishment. I spent as little time at home as possible.

Tenth grade ran the rest of its course uneventfully. I had one more operation to work on shaping the free-flap, which seemed as trivial and ineffectual to me as the last. I started spending a great deal of time privately looking at myself in the bathroom mirror. As before, I was willing to concede that the upper half of my face was indeed quite pretty, but I still felt it was completely negated by the lower half. Looking in the mirror, I would pull and push the various parts of my face I thought were ugly until I arrived at a facsimile of what I was *meant* to look like. When I'd finally find just the right angle and imagine how things were supposed to be, an intense sense of relief, and acceptance of myself, filled and lifted me.

Although I did not dare think such things to myself outwardly, I secretly hoped that once my face was fixed, my life would be fixed. This promise of beauty, which translated into a feeling of comfort and acceptance, would be constant and effortless, not something I had to conjure up distortedly in the bathroom mirror. Ugliness, the name I had given to fear and loneliness, would be just a distant memory. All I had to do was simply wait for my real face, my beautiful face, with as much dignity as I could muster. When I faltered, when some taunt or more subtle rejection depressed me, I comforted myself by telling myself that this wasn't my real face, just some curious mask. This face I saw in the mirror had nothing to do with me.

I spent every day that summer at the barn. One day too hot to get very much accomplished, I went with some people from the stable on an errand in the car. We got caught in traffic along the main road, and as we crept along at a snail's pace, I got lost in my own world, looking out of the window. A bakery storefront caught my attention, its door set at a very odd angle, reminding me of something I couldn't quite put my finger on. It was then I remembered that I had been to this town some ten or twelve years ago with my father. He loved to go out for a drive on a Sunday and explore the area, and Sarah and I always loved to accompany him. We'd stand up in the back seat and sing songs with him, songs from his own distant childhood, so familiar and lovely to him that we could both hear that strange, sad love in his voice as he sang. Unexpectedly, and consciously for the first time since his death, I longed for my father's presence. The whole time he'd been in the hospital, I'd only visited him once. At one point during that visit I went to wait outside in the hallway. The smells and sounds were so familiar, the sweet disinfectant and wax, always an aroma of overcooked food in the background, the metallic clinks of IV poles as they were pushed along the floor on their stands. Yet I was only visiting, passing through. I had felt alone and without purpose, unidentified, not sure how to act. I didn't know how to act now, either. I didn't want to ignore the grief or even get over it, because that would mean that I hadn't loved my father. When my horse died, I cried almost continuously for days. The loss was pure and uncomplicated. Loving my father had been a different matter. Over a year after his death, I finally and suddenly found myself consumed with a longing for his actual presence.

I started imagining my father standing next to me in the hospital, visiting me. Re-imagining with all my might, I strained to hear the background noises of the hospital, feel the starch of the sheets and hear my father's footsteps approaching me, hear the rustle of his clothes as he stood near me, his cough to see if I was awake. I'd imagine opening my eyes, very slowly, very carefully, and try to see him there, standing beside my hospital bed. All I could ever conjure was the vaguest of outlines, a passing detail which only seemed to obscure the rest of him: how his watch fitted on his wrist, how he would trace the edge of his ear with one finger.

Spending as much time as I did looking in the mirror every day, I thought I knew what I looked like. So it came as a shock one afternoon towards the end of that summer when I went shopping with my mother for a new shirt and saw my face in the harsh fluorescent light of the fitting room. Pulling the new shirt on over my head, I caught a glimpse of my reflection in a mirror which was itself being reflected in a mirror opposite, reversing my face as I usually saw it. I stood there motionless, the shirt only halfway on, my skin extra pale from the lighting, and saw how asymmetrical my face was. How had that happened? Walking up to the mirror, reaching up to touch the right side where the graft had been put in only a year ago, I saw clearly for the first time that most of it had disappeared, melted away into nothing. Sighting myself this way made me distraught, but not nearly as distraught as thinking of how long it had taken me to notice, to think my eye had been secretly working against me, making up for the asymmetry as it gradually developed, and that this, this reversed image of myself, was the true image, the way other people saw me.

I felt like such a fool. I'd been walking around with a secret notion of promised beauty, and there was the reality. I saw Dr Baker a few weeks later and wanted desperately to ask him what had gone wrong, but found myself speechless. Besides, I knew the graft had reabsorbed, had simply been taken back by my body. The doctor had warned me it might happen. He spoke of waiting a few years before trying any more big operations, of letting me grow some more. We spoke about a series of minor operations, fidgety little ones that would make readjustments to what was already there, but there was only vague talk of any new grafts, of putting more soft tissue or bone in place. Sitting there in his expensively decorated office, I felt utterly powerless. Realizing I was going to have to change my ideals and expectations was one thing, but knowing what to replace them with was another.

Seeing myself so unexpectedly in that store's fitting room mirror marked a turning point in my life. I began having overwhelming attacks of shame. They came at unpredictable intervals. The first one came as I was speaking to Hans, my boss at the stable. He was describing how he wanted me to ride a certain horse. I was looking him in the eye as he spoke, he was looking me in the eye. Out of nowhere came the overwhelming feeling that he shouldn't be looking at me, that I was too horrible to look at, that I wasn't worthy of being looked at, that my ugliness was equal to a great personal failure. Inside, I was churning and shrinking, desperate for some course of action to follow to get me out of this. I took the only course of action I knew I was any good at. I acted as if nothing were wrong at all. Steadying myself, breathing deep, I kept looking him in the eye, determined that he should know nothing of what I was thinking.

That summer I started riding horses for Hans in local schooling shows. I always rode wearing a helmet with my hair hanging loose beneath it, but etiquette required that while I was actually showing my hair had to be placed neatly up beneath the helmet, out of sight. I put this off until the very last minute, trying to act casual as I reached for the rubber-band and hairnet. For some reason this simple act of lifting my hair and exposing my face was among the hardest things I ever had to do. As hard as facing Dr Woolf, harder than facing operations: I would have gladly exchanged any amount of physical pain to keep my hair down. No one at the show grounds ever commented to me about it, and certainly no one here was going to make fun of me, but I was beyond that point. Yet it was somehow easier to face actual pain, as in the case of chemo or surgery, or cope with emotional pain such as the grief over my father's death. I was merely putting my hair up. No one had to make fun of me, or judge me, because by then I was perfectly capable of doing it all by myself.

The habits of self-consciousness, of always looking down and hiding my face behind my hair or my hand, were so second-nature by now that I was blind to them. When my mother pointed these habits out to me in the hope of making me stop, telling me they directed even more attention to my face, it was as if she were telling me to change the colour of my eyes. I fantasized about break-throughs in reconstructive surgery, about winning the lottery and buying my own private island, about being abducted by space aliens who'd fix me up and plop me back down in the midst of a surprised public. And there were still acts of heroism out there waiting to be thrust upon me, whole busloads of babies to be saved and at least one, there had to be at least one out there, wise older man who'd read about my heroism in the papers, who'd fall in love with my inner beauty and whisk me away from the annoyance of existence as defined by Spring Valley High School.

Throughout the eleventh and twelfth grades, I underwent several small operations. The hospital was the only place on earth where I didn't feel self-conscious. On the contrary, my face was my battle scar, my badge of honour. The plastic surgery ward was full of people getting their noses done, their faces lifted. They hated their gorgeously hooked noses, their wise lines, their exquisitely thin lips. Beauty, as defined by society at large, seemed to be only about who was best at looking like everyone else. If *I* had a face that was my original face, an undamaged face, *I* would know how to appreciate it, know how to see the beauty of it. Yet each time I was wheeled down to the surgical wing, high on the drugs, I'd think to myself, *Now, now I can start my life, just as soon as I wake up from this operation*. And no matter how disappointed I felt when I did wake up and look in the mirror, I'd just postpone happiness until the next operation. That was one thing I could rely on, that there would always be another operation, another chance for my life finally to begin.

It was in the wake of this disappointment that I'd often chide myself for thinking I'd ever be beautiful enough, good enough, or worthy enough of someone else's love, let alone my own. Who cared if I loved my own face or not if no one else was going to? What was beauty for, after all, if not to attract the attention of men, of lovers? Walking down a street or hallway, sometimes men would whistle at me from a distance, call me Baby, yell out and ask me my name. I was thin, I had a good figure, and my long blonde hair, when I bothered to brush it, was pretty. But I knew what was coming and would walk as fast as possible, my head bent down, but sometimes they'd catch up with me, or I'd be forced to pass by them. Their comments would stop instantly when they saw my face, their sudden silence potent and damning.

Life, mankind in general, was cruel and offered only different types of voids and chaos. The only way to tolerate it, to have any hope of escaping it, I reasoned, was to know my own strength, to defy life by surviving it. Sitting in maths class, I'd look around and try to gauge who among my classmates could have lived through this trauma, certain none of them could. I had already read a great deal about the Holocaust, but now we were reading first-person accounts by Eli Weisel and Primo Levi in social studies. I was completely transported by their work and the more I absorbed of their message, the more my everyday life took on a surreal quality. Now everything, *everything*, seemed important. The taste of salt and peanut butter and tomatoes, the smell of car fumes, the small ridge of snow that rested on the inside sill of a barely open window. I thought that this, then, was how to live in the now moment, to re-see the world: continuously imagine a far worse reality. The life I was leading, at these moments, seemed so utterly unimportant, uncomplicated. Sometimes I could genuinely find refuge in the world of my own private senses, but just as often I disingenuously affected a posture of repose, and used it only as a weapon against people I envied and feared, as a way of feeling superior to and thus safe from them.

After the section on the Holocaust, my social studies class moved onto art history. One day I walked in late and the lights were off. My teacher was just about to show slides. Giacometti's sculptures flashed on the wall, their elongated arms simultaneously pointing both towards and away from the world, while their long legs held them tall and gracefully, but tenuously. Next were Di Chirico's, with their shadows from unseen others falling directly across the paths of the visible. I had seen Munch's 'The Scream' before and had identified it with my own occasional desire to let out a howl, but it was only at that moment, sitting in that darkened classroom, that I understood the figure might not be screaming himself, but shielding his ears from and dropping his mouth open in shock at the sound of someone, or something else's, loud, loud lament. Right after that came Matisse's paintings, which seemed to me all about how simple and easy it was to see the world in a beautiful way. And after that, there were Picasso's, which were about how equally complex, how equally difficult, beauty was.

In English class poems had similar effects on me. My taste was not always sophisticated, but I did read poems by Keats, Emily Dickinson and Wallace Stevens which moved me in ways I couldn't understand. It was, in part, this very lack of understanding which was so moving. I would read a poem, Keat's 'Ode To A Nightingale', and feel that something important, something necessary was being said here, but the moment I tried to examine the words, dissect the sentences, the meaning receded.

Senior year I applied to and got accepted by Sarah Lawrence College with a generous scholarship. Not exactly sure what else to do with my life, I decided to work towards medical school. The day senior class yearbook photos were taken I purposefully cut school, and threw away all the subsequent notices I received warning that unless I attended the make-up shoot, my photo would not appear in the yearbook.

11
Cool
====

CERTAIN PEOPLE GO through radical outward changes in their freshman year of college. This is especially true at Sarah Lawrence, with an enrolment of only eight hundred people and a decidedly liberal arts oriented programme. It was only an hour from Spring Valley, and my mother drove me there, helped me carry my boxes up to my dorm room and, after saying goodbye, drove away. From all the way across the parking lot outside my window I could hear a Herman's Hermits song blaring out 'Something tells me I'm into something good'. I took it as an omen. For days beforehand I'd been a nervous wreck, but suddenly I felt I belonged. It was an unusual, curious feeling.

Sarah Lawrence is something of a satellite for New York City's lower east side. Everyone I met seemed to be either dressed entirely in black or sporting bizarre haircuts indicating the over-zealous use of a razor blade, while others wore with enviable grace and style exotic, ruined clothes that looked as if they'd washed up on shore after the *Titanic*'s New Year's Eve party. Everyone cultivated an air of being an outsider, of being beyond it all, of being utterly cool. Being rather naive, I fell for these appearances instantly, was completely seduced by them, and was shocked to discover that rather than snubbing me, everyone was extraordinarily nice and even interested in me. After unpacking my belongings I went to the first official and unofficial meetings and was amazed to observe myself so at ease, so ready and able to make contact with people. Though I'd had some friends before college, they were people I spent time with more than actual friends, people I would never consider showing my private self to. It was different here. Within hours I was having intense discussions about life, art, all the stuff I'd been craving for so long.

Yet, for all these deep conversations, how one looked still seemed to be of tantamount importance. Only the aesthetic had changed. In many ways the fashion of cool was every bit as rigorous and unforgiving as the fashion of fitting-in had been in high school, only here the rigours depended upon a higher degree of individuality. With amazing predictability, predictability we the inductees of cool would have scorned had anyone tried to point it out to us, the freshman class went through its first semester transformations. I was no exception.

Some of us arrived back on campus after Thanksgiving break, our embarrassing old chinos and docksiders left at home, completely vamped out in retro-punk: dyed magenta hair and green fingernails and long black skirts. Others went for the style of oversized dressed from their grandmother's closets, strange little hats with feathers, and pearl necklaces that hung to their navels. Still others went for the sex-toy look: ripped jeans over lace stockings and tee shirts with collars and sleeves tantalizingly torn off. Not surprisingly, I went with the I-don't-care-I'm-an-artist-look, which required everything I wore to come from the Bargain Box, the local thrift store, and cost no more than a dollar fifty. Extra points went to anything I found lying on the street.

At the heart of this anti-fashion statement was poetry. Still set on going to medical school, I had signed up for the required science courses, but had needed to fill out my schedule with something in the humanities. My mother urged me to take one of the writing workshops the school is well known for and, deciding that fiction would be too much work, I opted for a poetry course. My instructor was a man named John Skoyles and by the end of the first semester I was hooked.

Poetry, and the writing of poetry, brought together everything which had ever been important to me. I could dwell in the realm of the senses as before, but now there was a discipline, a form for them. Rather than a way of creating my own private life and shunning the world, the ability to perceive was now a way to enter the world. Language itself, words and images, could be wrought and shaped into vessels for the truth and beauty I had so long hungered for. Most amazingly, one could fail, one could make mistake after mistake and still learn from them.

Poetry became a religion for me. I was a fanatic. I'd pull people into corners and tell them, without any sense of irony, 'You have to hear this, it will change your life.' I'd recite anything from Rilke to Ashberry, certain that the deep wonder and awe I felt for these poems would be immediately apparent. I recognized this wonder and awe as intimately connected to the feelings I'd discovered while recovering from the chemotherapy sessions, when just simply to 'be' was reason enough for joy. With hindsight, I recognized that joy as a kind of fearlessness, a falling away of expectations that the world should be anything other than what it was. And now, I thought, I'd at last discovered the means with which to seek out actively this kind of being, this kind of beauty.

By the end of my freshman year I'd gained something of a reputation as one of the better poets on campus. This aided in the development of my artistic persona. How trivial actually to *think* about one's appearance. For my fellow scruffy artists, their less-than-casual attire was an indication to the world that it should recognize them as geniuses too preoccupied with their own genius to care for something as mundane as clothes. But for me, dressing as if I didn't care was an actual attempt not to care, to show the world I wasn't concerned with what it thought of my face. Dressing in my carefully orchestrated shabbiness, I was hoping to beat the world to the finish by showing that I knew I was ugly first. Still, all the while, I was secretly hoping that in the process some potential lover might accidentally notice I was wearing my private but beautiful heart on my stained and fraying sleeve.

In truth there was little danger of meeting someone who might actually desire me, and not just because of my looks. The female-to-male ratio at school was three to one, and the third of the population that was male was, for the most part and for varying reasons, unavailable. As it was, I was free to develop my eccentric ways and thoughts without the threat of undermining my most basic assumptions about myself, my most intimate definitions of what constituted my personality, however painful those definitions might otherwise have been.

That summer I was looking forward to going into the hospital to have a second free-flap attempted, but it wasn't to be. My mother had to leave her job at the nursing home, which meant I no longer had medical insurance. Plus, to ease her financial burden, she decided to sell the house, which demanded a great deal of repair and general sorting out. After weeks of filling out forms and spending hours on the telephone on hold, I eventually received Medicaid. I went to see Dr Baker and together we decided to postpone surgery for the following summer, as this summer was already half over.

The house was sold early that fall of my sophomore year. For years our poor old dilapidated house had been nothing but an embarrassment, and I'd underestimated the value of it as a reliable source of comfort, as a place I could always go. Now, to my surprise, I missed it. I experienced a strange kind of orphanhood, a displacement which worked its way into my aesthetics. The word 'home' kept cropping up in my poems. When school vacations came around, I'd often spend them as the guest of friends instead of in my mother's new smaller apartment. As opposed to high school, I now possessed a large number of varied and decidedly wonderful friends I valued immeasurably.

Through them, I discovered what it was to love people. There was an art to loving them, I discovered, which was not really all that different from the love that was necessary in the making of art. It required an effort of always seeing them for themselves and not what I wished them to be, of always striving to see the truth of them. My vanity allowed me to be proud of the different types of friends I possessed. I was on equally good terms with radically political and openly hedonistic people, friends who were concerned deeply with the spiritual and those who couldn't care less about it. Generally, they didn't mix with each other, and often each of them was sincerely surprised to discover that I spent time outside their own group, though for the most part all of them shared the quality of being on the fringe. To be on the fringe at a school as fringy as Sarah Lawrence was itself an accomplishment, but it was this very quality that I loved most about my friends. They wore their mantles as 'outsiders' with pride, whether it was because of their politics, their sexuality or anything else which can make a person feel outside of the norm. Their self-definition was the very thing which put me at ease with them. I didn't feel judged. I felt an acceptance I had never experienced before and was able genuinely to open myself to the love offered.

As the close of sophomore year drew near, I went to see Dr Baker about setting up the next operation. I was full of hope, but things seemed to be turning out differently than planned. Dr Baker had far too much work right then to do the operation himself, and was handing me over to two other surgeons who worked out of St Vincent's Hospital, down in Greenwich Village. While I was waiting in Dr Baker's office, these two new doctors walked in, examined me, and left. Dr Baker assured me that this team was very capable.

Free-flaps are all-day operations, six or eight hours long, and I felt somehow that I should be understanding of how much time it would take, that I should just go along and let these strange doctors take over. 'I'm still your doctor,' he assured me, but I felt completely cowed and didn't have a right to speak up and voice my fears. I wanted to know if this change in affairs had anything to do with being on Medicaid now, but I felt too stupid to ask.

Things didn't go well right from the start. I went to St Vincent's in the midst of a heat wave, and the air conditioning in my room, with its permanently shut windows was broken. I had the operation and woke up in sweat beneath the sheets. Still delirious and in intense pain, I pulled the stiff sheets off me only to see that rather than the normal line of stitches I had expected to see along my hip, where they'd taken the graft from, there was a long row of thirty or forty large metal staples. It looked as if someone had sawed my leg off and then put it back on with an office stapler. The sight of it upset me, but when I tried to speak, I found they'd given me a tracheotomy, another surprise.

Coming out of eight hours of anaesthesia takes a long time and is not a pleasant process. I kept surfacing into consciousness, taking note of one detail, such as the staples, then sinking back down again, only to re-emerge a while later with no sense of how much time had passed, where I was, what on earth was happening. I couldn't understand why I had staples in my leg, and I was never coherent enough or conscious long enough to figure it out, to know it was simply an experiment in wound closure. I kept hallucinating gruesome scenes in which nurses were attacking me with pliers. My whole body kept shaking, and I found I could not stop crying, even though it did not seem to me that I was the one crying: it was as if I were watching a movie of someone else lying in a bed, trembling and crying. I felt like a small child. I didn't feel safe.

At some point in the night I realized it was difficult for me to breathe. I wrote out a note to the nurse, who said she would tell the doctor. An hour later, it was getting worse, I had to think about every breath. I wrote another note to the nurse and finally a doctor arrived to draw an arterial blood sample to check my oxygen level. I don't know how much time went by, but it was still dark, the night seemed so long, there didn't seem to be any people around. I was frightened. The doctor came in again and started taking another blood sample. I was only dimly aware of him. I didn't seem to be able to see anything very clearly and his voice sounded muffled as he said hello to another doctor who walked in and asked him, 'Didn't you just do a blood gas a little while ago?' I could hear them talking as if through water. 'Yeah', he replied congenially, 'but I couldn't believe anyone's oxygen level could be that low.' However unable I was to communicate with the outside world, this comment jolted my inside voice awake. Oh my God, I thought to myself, brain damage. I'm going to have brain damage, I'm going to be brain-dead, and as far as I could tell, no one seemed really to care all that much.

I lay in bed and focused on someone's hand resting on the end-rail of my bed. Several people were having a conversation about what to do with me but I couldn't concentrate on it, all I could think about was how cinematic this pale hand looked, resting there on its wrist, limply, letting its fingers point towards the sheets. Sometimes it would twitch up, even turn its palm upward a little, like any hand would when its owner was making a point. Then it was lifted up and taken away and someone stepped up next to me and leaned down to tell me they were going to take me to Intensive Care, that I was going to be put on a respirator.

Now this, I thought to myself, sounds like an excellent idea. Finally I'll be able to breathe. My few belongings were taken out of the bedside cabinet, put into a plastic bag and plopped on the bed near my feet. The brakes were lifted off the bed's wheels and off we went, me in a bed pushed by a nurse and a student doctor. The hospital seemed deserted and we actually got lost two times, the nurse and student doctor arguing about which hallway to go down, blaming each other like an old married couple. Now that I was a bit more relaxed, knowing there was a respirator in my future, I saw some comic aspects to my predicament.

I was finally put on the respirator, and it was discovered that I had pneumonia. I spent a hellish week in Intensive Care, where the lights were on twenty-four hours a day, the air conditioning was still broken and every once in a while the alarm on my heart monitor would go off for no apparent reason. It was very loud and always jolted me right off the sheets. I always had to wait for someone to come and give it a whack, as if it was a television, before it would stop. Most oddly, though, it seemed everyone was speaking very peculiarly to me. I couldn't put my finger on just what was so bizarre about their speech (was I on some strange sort of drug?) until finally a male nurse I'd never seen before very slowly and with over-exaggerated movements of his mouth asked, 'How long did it take you to learn lip-reading?' For some inexplicable reason, they thought I was deaf. Later that day a crew of workmen came and started ripping down the wall only a few feet away from the foot of my bed in order to fix some pipes. Their jackhammers made my metal bed-rails jingle and set my heart monitor off again.

I had been so ill while in the hospital that I hadn't been able to put much effort into thinking about my appearance. My mother had been loaned the use of an apartment on the upper east side for the summer and I went to stay there with her. One whole side of the living-room was covered with mirrors. I walked into the apartment and almost fainted at the sight of me. The graft hadn't been applied to just one side of my face, but ran from one ear to the other and was obscenely swollen to the size of a football. A very large piece of pale skin from my hip had been left in, not just a small patch like last time. This strip was a foot long and four inches wide, and on either side of it were long rows of sutures. If feeling like a freak had been more in my mind than in my face at other times in my life, this visage I saw staring back at me was undeniably repulsive. The feeling was confirmed for me whenever I went out on the street. People would stop in their tracks and stare at me. One afternoon a beggar ran up behind me, demanding money. I stopped and turned around to look at him. He stopped in mid-sentence, looked at me for a second longer, then politely apologized and handed me a dollar bill before turning away, muttering something to himself. My self-esteem reached the bottom of the deepest, darkest pit.

I was promised a revision operation before going back to school and I placed all my hope on that. Maybe it wasn't really so bad after all, I tried to tell myself, the swelling would eventually go down and and the skin would be taken away. I simply had to accept that and try my best to make use of the time spent waiting, to numb any and all desires to look normal. I spent a lot of time sitting alone in the dark kitchen which had only one small lightless window, sweating from the heat and giving myself pep talks, diatribes on the truer meaning of life.

One afternoon still early in the summer the phone rang. It was Steven, one of my friends from college. When he asked me how I was I tried to answer, but all that came out was choking tears. 'Hang on,' he said, 'I'm coming to get you.' An hour later the bell rang and when I opened the door, I expected to have to go into a long discussion about why I looked the way I did, but before I even started Steven announced we were going dancing that night. Dancing? Was he serious? He was. He had only just come out as a homosexual, and he told me I was the only one he trusted enough to accompany him to the gay clubs. It was important, he said, he was counting on me to support him.

My own sexuality completely on hold, I found myself in a world comprised of sex. I felt both safe and amazed by this sudden proximity to dozens of half-naked men suggestively grinding their hips on the dance floor. The club was called The Monster, and the sex here had nothing to do with me. No one took any notice of me, I was without value in this world. It was easy to sublimate my own desire, and sustain my feelings of physical worthlessness. I put all my energy into learning to dance. My teachers were some of the great anonymous masters of the mid-eighties dance club scene. I spent my first few visits simply watching before finally getting up enough nerve to go out on the floor myself. Never in a million years would I have been able to do this in a heterosexual club, but here, what the hell? I learned the balance between letting loose and keeping control, allowing my body to react impulsively to the beat

and directing that impulse into a more meditated, skilled movement. It was all about rhythm, about finding the place where the
music's rhythm met my own, and as I danced away I would think
how this wasn't all that different from making art. Every once in a
while I would think, fleetingly, this must also be what it was like to
act sexually in the world. But mostly I just treated the whole thing
academically.

In senior year I became friends with a group of transvestites I'd
met in the clubs. They took me under their wing. Lying back on a
clothes-strewn bed, I'd spend long evenings watching as they
prepared to go out, a process which could last for hours. Their
notions of beauty were extreme: gobs of make-up, technicolour
dresses, and most crucial of all, they tried to impress upon me, the
art of accessorizing. Sometimes my friends would literally drag me
off the bed and gather round to play with me, experimenting with
different make-up techniques. They put on such absurd amounts,
everything from foundation to lipstick to false eyelashes. Looking
at myself in the mirror, there was little danger of having to think of
myself as being a 'real' girl, about doing real girl things. I'd been
going after the androgynous effect, and with my slight figure
shrouded in baggy clothes, I was often mistaken for a boy. I felt
very safe dressed this way. As I watched my friends dress up, I felt
very far away from my own femininity.

I relished the eccentrics in my life. I seemed to know a lot of
them, and through a snowball effect to attract more of them all the
time. A friend of a friend introduced me to Divine, the famous
female impersonator, and I found myself at parties populated by
the likes of Andy Warhol, famous fashion designers and erstwhile
rock stars. They rarely gave me much more than a passing glance,
but I felt a strange sense of belonging within these crowds of
people, all of us so excessively bound to the world of appearance.
At night I went to all the hippest of the hip clubs and danced myself
into a frenzy.

Walking around these dark clubs, I felt the same strange power I
used to feel among the parents I had encountered at the pony
parties. As long as I disengaged any expectations of being
physically desired by anyone, I was able to indulge a fantasy of
myself as an artist, as someone special, a face you remembered.

*

The summer came to an end, the grotesque swelling came down and I had a revision operation. Though I didn't feel particularly good about my image, I didn't actually feel bad about it either. This in itself was a momentous step forward, and I decided to push myself one step further. I cut my hair. I knew it was the only way I would ever stop hiding behind it. Starting off with a long bob, I worked in small stages, every few weeks making it shorter and shorter until by the end of my junior year it was only a few inches long. During that year the free-flap was slowly reabsorbed like the last one. Once again I had nothing to show for the operation but the scarred donor site. Finally, the summer before my final year at college, I was scheduled for a bone graft.

The graft would be non-vascularized, meaning a lump of bone would be taken from my hip, ground up and then, like clay, fashioned into the rough shape of a jaw. For the first time, the effect of an operation was immediate and remarkable because bone doesn't swell. I remember limping out of bed to the bathroom and not believing my own eyes as I swung open the door. Could that really be me? For weeks afterwards I kept putting my hand up and checking to make sure it was still there, an actual jaw. For the first time in memory, I actually looked forward to looking in the mirror, seeing a face I liked.

What was puzzling to me was that I still didn't feel attractive, despite what all my friends were telling me. Wasn't all my fear just supposed to fall away, wasn't someone supposed to fall in love with me, wasn't life supposed to *work* now? Where was all that relief and freedom that I thought came with beauty?

12

Mirrors

THE GENERAL PLOT of life is sometimes shaped by the different ways genuine intelligence combines with equally genuine ignorance. I put all my effort into looking at the world as openly, unbiasedly and honestly as possible, but I could not recognize my own self as a part of this world. I took great pains to infuse a sense of grace and meaning into everything I saw, but I could not apply those values to myself. Personally, I felt meaningless, or, more precisely, I felt I meant nothing to anyone.

Even though I now possessed many rich friendships, had people who valued me, not having a lover meant I was ultimately unlovable. What I didn't realize, however, was what a major step forward it was for me to begin to own my desires. But rather than finding affirmation in knowing my friends loved me, I turned it against myself: if so many people thought I was such a lovable person, the fact that I still wasn't able to get a lover proved them wrong. Whatever sense of inner worth I developed was eroded by the knowledge that I could only compensate for, but never overcome the obstacle of my face.

I realized that I was consumed with self-pity, but try as I might I couldn't shake it. Because I had grown up depriving myself of any feeling that vaguely resembled self-pity, I now had to find a way to reshape it. Just as I had been comforted by the Christian pamphlets which arrived at our home, I found myself reading the bible, though I could not find it within myself to believe. I read the Old and New Testament and recognized in them a certain movement of time, a cycle of mourning that began with an expulsion and moved towards a reconciliation. It was the dynamic of my own life, reaffirmed in a different language. I read different philosophers and imagined my soul, separate and clear of my heart and mind. Other times I was so lonely I was amazed I didn't just expire right there on the spot, as if loneliness that strong was equal to a divine thunderbolt that could strike me down at any moment, whether I was on my own bed, at a crowded dinner table, or an empty roadside stop.

Not surprisingly, I saw sex as my salvation. If only I could get someone to have sex with me, then that would mean I was attractive, that someone could love me. I never doubted my own ability to love someone, only that it would never be returned. The longing for someone and the fear that there would never be anyone intermingled to the point where I couldn't tell the difference. My longing itself, my neediness, transformed itself into a firm belief that my love would never be reciprocated. Even though it was obvious that the major reason I was still a virgin when I graduated from college was the dearth of genuine opportunities combined with a crippling lack of self-esteem, I persisted in seeing this as proof that I had lost out on the world of love simply and only because of my looks.

All of this would change when I went to graduate school. I had long given up on the idea of going to medical school and instead applied to MFA programmes for poetry. If sex wasn't going to be my salvation, writing and poetry would. But within two days of arriving in Iowa I met the man who would become my first lover. There was no doubt I was an easy mark, and on the surface Jude was everything I imagined I wanted: he was an older, handsome writer who drove antique sports cars and had an unusual name and a quirky personality. He had lived a difficult, interesting life. On the whole he was, as he loved to hear me describe him, terribly dashing.

The relationship was a disaster. I never for a moment thought I was in love with Jude or that he was in love with me, but it was a highly charged sexual relationship. At last I had found someone who was attracted to me, and I allowed his attraction to define me. At his prompting, I began dressing more like 'a woman', despite the fact that I still could not bring myself to use the personal pronoun and the word woman in the same sentence. At first I felt like an impostor, but as time wore on even I had to admit I had a sexy body. I went from looking like a boy to wearing miniskirts, garter belts and high heels. Once I started dressing provocatively I couldn't stop. It was just as much a costume as dressing androgynously had been, and even though these new dresses hid none of my curves, I believed they hid my fear of being ugly. I thought I could use my body to distract people from my face. It made me feel worthy. I couldn't even go to the supermarket without getting dressed up.

All of this parading around didn't hide the fact that the bone graft was slowly going the way of all the other grafts. I didn't really notice it until the day after Jude broke up with me. Looking in the mirror, I saw the telltale signs of what was beginning to happen and felt a huge dread come over me. It had all been a lie. I had fooled Jude into thinking I was something other than I was, and now reality was slowly and indefatigably manifesting itself again. This is when I began dressing in earnest slinkiness. I began spending two hours a day at the gym, imposing a killer regime on myself. This was one thing which I had control over. If I had put even a tenth of the energy I spent obsessing over my face and my body into my work, I could have written *War and Peace* ten times over.

Bent on proving I was desirable, I started collecting lovers, having a series of short-term relationships that always ended, I was absolutely certain, because I wasn't beautiful enough. I became utterly convinced that anyone who might want to have a real relationship with me was automatically someone I didn't want. It was the classic Groucho Marx paradox: I didn't want to belong to any club that would have me as a member.

Dr Baker and I decided to try another soft-tissue free-flap. So much of the original irradiated tissue had been replaced with non-irradiated tissue that he felt there was a good chance this graft would stick. A few months prior to having the operation, I discovered, due to an accumulation of details ranging from the fact that I did not live in the state the operation was to be performed in to the fact I was a full-time student with a teaching fellowship, Medicaid would not pay my hospital bills. I had to put the operation off until the following summer.

At Dr Baker's suggestion I went to the University of Iowa hospital for a consultation with the head of plastic surgery, who was an old friend of his. Perhaps there was a way of having him do the operation. Iowa's Medicaid system was on a first-come first-serve funding basis. I could not apply for funding before the operation: I had to go and have it, submit the bills and hope there was enough left in the budget to pay for it. I wasn't very optimistic about the whole thing when I went for my appointment.

The surgeon was from the old school. Of course my free-flaps had shrunk, he told me, they always did. He suggested sticking with the old pedestal method that Dr Conley had outlined for me so many years ago. He was very enthusiastic, explaining in far greater detail than Conley had about all the different incisions he'd make. He described how I could spend the six weeks my hand was sewn to my stomach and then to my face in the hospital, and that while my hand was sewn to my face he would rig me up with a special cast to hold everything in place. He even introduced me to a patient of his who was having a pedestal to rebuild his nose. This patient's nose had been shot off with a gun, and he was sporting a very complicated and uncomfortable looking cast which was forcibly holding his own wrist to his face. Connecting his wrist to the area of his nose was a pale tube of skin with a red row of sutures down the side. I felt utterly repulsed, and I felt ashamed of my repulsion.

After this patient had left and not wanting to be rude, I calmly told the surgeon that I probably couldn't do this after all because of the money involved. 'Oh, don't let that worry you. You wait right here.' He disappeared for a long fifteen minutes, leaving me alone in the office. I decided this was as good a time as any to see if it was possible to have an out-of-body experience. Having read only in passing about out-of-body experiences, and these mostly in supermarket tabloids, I mistakenly thought you were supposed to follow an actual physical route, so I closed my eyes and tried imagining what the air duct over my head might look like if I were inside it.

Eventually the surgeon returned with a hospital financial officer, who outlined the payment plan for the three major operations and the minor follow-up, and the cost of the extended in-patient stays. When he had finished his calculations, he assured me that with monthly payments of only a hundred dollars I could pay the original bill and all the accumulated interest off by the time

I was forty-two. He was very affable and I shook his hand, telling him I'd think about it.

I stayed calm until I reached the street outside, when I broke into a run and didn't let up until I got home four miles away. Once home, I started to hyperventilate. I was even more upset that my own body should betray me now, just when I needed it to hang on most. There was no way I was going to put myself through those operations, let alone have the pleasure of paying them off just when I should be rightfully starting my mid-life crisis along with everybody else.

There I was with my short skirts and sharp mind and list of lovers, trying so hard to convince myself that maybe all I really needed to do was learn how to treat myself better. I was on the verge of feeling this way, yet I was still so suspicious, still so certain that only someone else's love could prove it absolutely. Forget all that now, though, because here was the ugly truth. I felt I had been shown a mirror of what my life really was, what I really was, and I simply did not want to look. I was someone who doctors talked to about sewing her hand to her face. I was someone trying to believe there really wasn't all that much wrong with her after all, but here were my worst suspicions, confirmed.

Lying in my usual abject heap on the living-room carpet, a pose I often adopted in dire times, I mouthed the words 'I'm tired. I don't want to do this any more.' For the very first time, I didn't adopt either a noble or catastrophic interpretation of the events. For so long I'd been hell-bent on accepting everything that had happened to me, on trying to devise some grand scheme of meaning, that the mere thought of simply rejecting everything felt akin to heresy. It was reality after all: I did have cancer once, I did have a disfigured face now, there was no denying these two things. I felt pulled in two different directions. I had tasted what it might be like to feel loved, to feel whole, and I had liked that taste. But fear kept insisting I needed concrete proof in the form of someone else's longing to believe in that love. Somehow I always boiled every equation down to these simple terms no matter how philosophical my ideals: was I lovable, or was I ugly?

As radical a decision as it was for me not to make a decision, simply not to *try* to reach a conclusion, I still knew that one way or another I would have an operation. This, I felt, was still beyond my control. After a great deal of finagling I managed to find funding for the next free-flap from a charity which came out of the New York University Center for Reconstructive Surgery. Dr Baker did the operation that summer and it was the usual story of hope and disappointment. I looked horrendous for a few months, then I looked better, and just as I was getting used to the new face, it started changing again, the graft started disappearing. I thought about trying another bone graft, but when I discovered that funds were limited, that there was only a finite number of times I could apply, I decided to give it up. This was me, this was my face, like it or lump it.

I opted for a geographic cure and decided to go live in Europe once school was finished. I took on extra jobs, worked around the clock and in a few months saved two thousand dollars and bought a ticket to Berlin. An old college friend was living there and that seemed as good a reason as any to pick that particular destination.

West Berlin, The Wall still intact at the time, fuelled every sentimental notion I had about living the bohemian life. I lived in a flat heated by giant pre-war porcelain ovens and no proper bathroom. Each morning I bathed in the kitchen sink. I applied for jobs teaching English at the various schools, and went for very cheap lessons in Kruezberg, a poor and rundown area near the Wall, to learn German along with a room full of Turkish immigrants. While waiting to hear about jobs, I spent my days sitting in the cafés, trying to write the ultimate poem about beauty and truth while simultaneously plotting to get rich from writing the great transatlantic trashy novel.

Living in a country where I didn't speak the language suited me just fine. Everything was an adventure, including buying milk at the corner store. I developed the art of getting lost. I'd intend to ride one U-Bahn line but often end up God knows where, a completely different part of town, with only my own wits and the help of strangers to get me back home. It was a safe kind of chaos, and at some point I understood that I was cultivating my 'aloneness' in this strange place as a method for putting off loneliness.

*

I maintained a romantic picture of myself as an ex-pat artist in Berlin for as long as possible, but work possibilities fell through and running low on funds I decided to go to London to live with my sister. I figured I'd find work more readily there since I spoke the language.

Normally, cities offered me a sense of anonymity, but everything felt different in London. Though I'd toned my fashion sense down quite a bit since Iowa, I still enjoyed wearing clothes that showed off my figure. Groups of men, usually young and usually drunk, would spot me from a distance and follow me, cat-calling. It was like junior high school all over again. As soon as they got nearer, near enough to see my face clearly, they'd start teasing me, calling me ugly, thinking it hysterically funny to challenge one another to ask me out on a date. I always stayed calm, kept right on walking, keeping my composure, but it was exhausting. I knew it had to do with their being drunk, that they would have targeted anyone in their path, that I just happened to be in the wrong place at the wrong time, but none of this helped.

One evening after I'd come home visibly upset from some teasing, my sister brought up a surgeon named Oliver Fenton whom she'd read about. He was working with a new method for plastic surgery known as a Tissue Expander. That had been while I was in Iowa, just after my last failed free-flap. She wrote to him and asked whether this new procedure might be of any benefit to me. He called her back himself and told her that he thought it might. When she called me from overseas, I was very doubtful.

People were always telling me about the 'wonderful things they can do today'. It was difficult explaining to people, even apologizing for the fact, that plastic surgery simply wasn't like the movies. There was never a dramatic moment when the bandages came off, nor a single procedure that would make it all alright. As soon as my sister had told me about this new doctor, I forgot all about him. Now, she brought him up again, how nice he'd sounded on the phone, and how it couldn't hurt to go and see him at least. He lived in Aberdeen, Scotland, seven hours by train from London. I couldn't afford the train ticket and in all likelihood I would have skipped it if Susie hadn't generously offered to buy the ticket as a present.

*

Fenton explained the whole procedure to me, which consisted of first inserting a tissue expander, to be followed by a vascularized bone graft. Because the bone graft would have its own blood supply, the chances of it reabsorbing were minimal. The procedure would take at least six months to finish; I knew enough about plastic surgery by then to know this probably meant a year. Telling him I'd think about it, I boarded the train back to London.

In the dining car I encountered yet another pack of drunken men more willing to judge my looks for me. I was frightened that none of Mr Fenton's proposed operations would work, that I would only be letting myself in for that familiar disappointment again. But, again but, how could I pass up the possibility that it might work, that at long last I might finally fix my face, fix myself, my life, my soul? And thanks to my European passport and the national medical services system, the operations would at least be free. Remembering the drunken but nonetheless cruel comments of those men on the train, I called up the doctor and told him yes.

An empty balloon was inserted under the skin on the right side of my face and then slowly blown up by daily injections of a few millilitres of saline into a special port beside my ear. The objective was to stretch out the skin slowly, much the way a pregnancy stretches the belly, so that there would be enough of my own skin to pull down and cover the bone graft. The whole process took about three months and I spent the entire time in the hospital. Everything else taken into consideration, I had a great time.

Everyone on the ward took it upon themselves to teach me about Scotland. The dialect was almost impenetrable at first, but I wasn't half bad by the time I left. Certain patients became good friends and, once they were released, took me for day trips to the beautiful countryside surrounding the town. The landscape brought up long-distant memories of Ireland. One of the doctors, a German woman named Eva, commiserated with me on our being foreigners and invited me home with her sometimes after work, sharing a good meal and making me feel special, not just like another patient.

I was happy to be in the hospital, relieved I didn't have to go out into the world looking this way. My face transformed on a daily basis into something rather monstrous. It was beginning to look as if a big balloon had been put in my face. I knew my appearance was strange, but there were other people with tissue expanders around me, other people on the ward worse off than myself, and I never felt the need to explain or apologize or feel ashamed about my appearance. Aware that physically I was capable of taking care of myself, that medically speaking there was no need for me to be an inpatient, it did not escape my attention that I was being treated like, equated with, a sick person simply because I did not look like other people.

The big day finally came and in what turned out to be an almost thirteen-hour operation due to some minor but unforeseen difficulties, the tissue expander was removed and the graft from my hip put in. I was severely disorientated when I woke up, a feeling exacerbated by the morphine that was being administered. The morphine didn't actually lessen the pain, rather it diminished my scope of awareness. As I kept waking and sinking back under I was overtaken by a brutal paranoia, convinced that because I had chosen to do this to myself, I deserved everything I got. Such long operations are rare and I don't think the staff were aware of this side effect: I was a complete wreck and no one knew to reassure me. It wasn't until Susie came up from London a couple of days later to visit me that the paranoia began to wear off. I don't think I'd ever been so happy to see someone in all my life.

I was very lame for a long time and tried not to think about the results. I knew there were more revision operations to come and I patiently waited for each of them. After several, my face was beginning to look acceptable to me, the new graft was solid and didn't seem in any jeopardy. But then something unexpected happened: the original bone on the left side, which had also been heavily irradiated, was starting to shrink, probably spurred on by all of the stress of such a large operation. I went in to see the doctor and he proposed putting a tissue expander in on the left side, followed by yet another free-flap.

I could not imagine going through it *again*, and just as I'd done all my life, I searched and searched for a way to make it okay, make it bearable, for a way to *do* it. I lay awake all night on a train back to London. I realized then that I had no obligation to improve my situation, that I didn't have to explain or understand it, that I could just simply let it happen. By the time the train pulled into King's Cross station I felt able to bear it yet again, not entirely sure what other choice I had.

I moved to Scotland, partly to be nearer the hospital and partly because I wanted more independence. Eligible for social security benefits, I was able to get my own, albeit very cold, flat, which overlooked a bridge under which whores congregated at night. It wasn't ideal, but it was mine. When I arrived at the hospital to set up a date to have the tissue expander inserted, I was informed that the procedure would take only three or four days. Almost in a whisper, I asked whether I was going to spend the whole expansion time in the hospital. I was told to come in every day to the outpatient ward to have it expanded instead. Horrified by this prospect, I left there speechless. I would have to live and move about in the outside world with a giant balloon stuck in my face. The next few days before I went into the hospital involved a great deal of drinking alone, both in bars and at home. I even picked someone up, a sweet and handsome man, probably every bit as lonely as I was. Lying next to him after it was over, I remember thinking I was fooling him, that he didn't have any idea who, or what, he was really with.

I went into the hospital, had the operation, and went home at the end of the week. The only things that gave me any comfort during the months I lived with my face gradually ballooning out were my writing and my reading. I wrote for hours and hours each day and lost myself reading everything from Kafka to Jackie Collins. I'd usually walk to the hospital, even though it was several miles. I didn't want to get on the bus and feel trapped that way, and luckily it was also cold, so I could wrap my whole head up in a scarf. As the tissue expander grew and grew this became harder to do. I stopped going out except to the hospital and to the little store round the corner from me to buy food. I knew the people who worked there from before, and I kept wondering when they were going to ask what was wrong. I assumed they thought I had some massive tumour and were afraid to ask.

Every time I went in there the lump was a little bit bigger, and finally I couldn't stand the polite silence any longer. I blurted out my whole life story to the man behind the counter. I was holding a glass bottle of milk, letting the whole saga stream out of me when the bells tied to the door jangled. A man I'd never seen before walked in. He was completely covered with tattoos. I stopped in mid-sentence and stared at him. He stopped in mid-stride and stared at me. There was a puma reaching across his cheek towards his nose, which had some kind of tree on it, the trunk of it running along the bridge and then flowering up on his forehead. There wasn't even one inch of naturally coloured skin: his ears, neck and hands were covered with lush jungle scenes and half-naked women with seashells covering their breasts.

I don't know why, but I felt immensely sorry for him. We finally broke our mutual stares, I paid for my milk, he bought a pack of cigarettes and we walked out together, turning different ways at the corner. In the same way that imagining living in Cambodia had helped me as a child, I walked the streets of my dark little Scottish city by the sea and knew without doubt that I was living in a story Kafka would have been proud to write.

The one good thing about the tissue expander is that you look so bad with it in that no matter what you look like once it's finally removed, it has to be better. I had the graft and some revised operations and by the summer, yes, even I had to admit I looked better. But I didn't look like me. Something was wrong: was *this* the face I had waited through eighteen years and almost thirty operations for? I just couldn't make what I saw in the mirror correspond to the person I thought I was. It wasn't only that I continued to feel ugly; I simply could not conceive the image as belonging to me. I had known this feeling before, but that had been when my face was 'unfinished', when there was still a large gap where my jaw should have been. But now there were no more major operations to be scheduled. There were still some minor ones, but for the most part, it was over. Was this it? How could this be? There was an impostor in the mirror, why couldn't anyone else see this?

I'd been through twelve operations in the three years I'd been living in Scotland: there was no denying Fenton was running out of things to do to me. But even as people confirmed this, even as people congratulated me, I felt I was being mistaken for someone else. That simply wasn't me in the mirror, and the only solution I could think of was to stop looking. It wasn't easy. I'd never suspected just how omnipresent our own images are. I became an expert on the reflected image, its numerous tricks and wiles, how it can spring up at you at any moment: a glass tabletop, a well-polished door handle, a darkened window, a pair of sunglasses, a restaurant's otherwise magnificent brass-plated coffee machine sitting innocently by the cash register. I perfected the technique of brushing my teeth without a mirror, grew my hair in such a way that it would require only a quick, simple brush, and wore clothes that were simply and easily put on, no complex layers or lines that might require even the most minor of visual adjustments. This went on for almost a year.

The journey back to my face was a long one. I had a few more minor operations and thanks to some unexpected money inherited from my grandmother, I travelled around Europe in between these operations. I kept writing. I returned to Berlin and sat in the same cafés as before, but now, without my image, without the frame-work of *when my face gets fixed, then I'll start living*. I felt there was something empty about me. I didn't tell anyone, not my sister, not my closest friends, that I had stopped looking in the mirror. I found that I could expertly look into a mirror and stare straight through it, allowing none of the mirror's reflection to get back to me. Unlike stroke victims who quite literally are unable to name the person in the mirror as themselves, my trick of the eye was the result of my lifelong refusal to learn *how* to name the person in the mirror. My face had been constantly changing for so long that there had never been time for me to become acquainted with it, develop anything other than an ephemeral relationship with it. It had been easy for me to develop beliefs about physical beauty, ascribe certain qualities to it which I thought I simply had to wait for. Now it was easier to think that I was still not beautiful enough or lovable enough than it was to admit that, perhaps, these qualities did not really belong to this thing I thought was called beauty after all.

Without another operation to hang all my hopes on, I found myself completely on my own. And somehow, something inside me started to miss me. There was a part inside me that organically *knew* I was whole, a part that had always been there. It was as if this part had known it was necessary to wait so long, to wait until the impatient din around it had quieted down, until the other internal voices had grown exhausted and hoarse before it could even begin to speak, before I would even begin to listen.

One evening near the end of my long separation from the mirror, I was sitting in a café talking to a man I found quite attractive when I suddenly wondered what I looked like to him. What was he *actually* seeing when he saw me? I sat there in the café and asked myself this old question, and startlingly, for the first time in my life, I had no ready answer prepared. I had not looked in a mirror for so long that I quite simply had no clue as to what I objectively looked like. I studied the man as he spoke; my entire life I'd handed my ugliness over to people and seen only the different ways it was reflected back to me. As reluctant as I was to admit it now, the only indication in my companion's behaviour was positive.

And then I experienced a moment of the freedom I'd been practising for behind my Halloween mask all those years ago. As a child I had expected my liberation to come as a result of getting a new face to put on, but now I saw that it was the result of shedding something, of shedding my image.

I used to think truth was an eternal, that once I *knew*, once I saw, this truth would be with me forever, a constant by which everything else could be measured. I know now this isn't so, that most truths are inherently unretainable, that we have to work hard all our lives to remember the most basic things. Society is no help. It tells us again and again that we can most be ourselves by acting and looking like someone else, only to leave our own original faces behind to turn into ghosts which will inevitably resent and haunt us. As I sat there in the café, it suddenly occurred to me that it is no mistake that sometimes in films and literature the dead only know they are dead after being offered that most irrefutable proof of all: they can no longer see themselves in the mirror.

Feeling the warmth of the cup against my palm, this small observation seemed like a great revelation to me. I wanted to tell the man I was with about it, but he was involved in his own thoughts and I did not want to interrupt him, so instead I looked with curiosity to the window behind him, its night-silvered glass reflecting the entire café, to see if I could, now, recognize myself.

I would like to thank the Bunting Institute of Radcliffe College, the Corporation of Yaddo, and the Fine Arts Work Center in Provincetown.